Foreword

by Bill McAllister

J Paul Getty's recipe for success was 'Rise early. Work hard. Strike oil.' David Sutherland didn't strike oil but you can substitute 'Think smart' for the recipe which has taken the boy brought up in a crowded Inverness council house to business success and a position where he could do so much good for others.

One of a railwayman's six children, David used his accountancy brain coupled with his business vision in two major deals. In 1989, he used his contacts, commercial acumen – and courage – to lead a management buyout which took Tulloch out of multinational hands and back into Highland ownership.

That was the firing pistol for rapid growth based on diversification. Housing and civil engineering divisions were added to the construction base of a company whose early business included making coffins!

As a result of that management buyout, jobs, good wages and careers were generated for literally thousands of Highland men and women. Tulloch's contribution to the Highlands and Islands economy has been significant.

Then in 2006, he sold the construction and civil engineering divisions to Rok plc for £31.6 million, a sign of how successful they had become under David's direction. He excluded Tulloch Homes from that deal and it remains the Highlands' largest housebuilder, a feat it achieved on the back of David's forthright accumulation of a major forward land bank.

His retiral in 2011 has seen him step up investment activities, including hotels and holiday lodges as well as a prime salmon stretch of the Ness.

He's such an active character that I was surprised he managed to find time to complete this book!

A sometimes overlooked element of the Sutherland makeup is that he retains a soft heart when it comes to helping others.

I have known him for some 30 years and have seen him donate to, and raise funds for, major charities such as Macmillan Cancer Care, Breast Cancer Scotland, the Princess Royal's Trust for Carers, the British Heart Foundation plus Highland Hospice and the Fort George Museum and Military Tattoo.

But other lesser known initiatives he has funded include transport for elderly people to their medical appointments, and other support for senior citizens, as well as helping Highland children with cancer to meet Phil Collins.

We've Come a Long Way

David Sutherland's history of his Tulloch Journey and beyond

All proceeds from this book will go to

Highland Children's Unit Appeal

THE ARCHIE FOUNDATION

MAKING THE DIFFERENCE FOR SICK CHILDREN IN RAIGMORE

A Charity for Children throughout the Highlands and Islands of Scotland

Cover picture by **Peter Jarvis**
Called "The Spark at Southampton Solent University"
http://pjarvis.co.uk/blog/

ISBN 978-1-910205-61-7

© **2015 David Sutherland**

ALL RIGHTS RESERVED

David Sutherland asserts his right under the Copyright,
Designs and Patents Act, 1988, to be identified
as the Author of this Work
British Library Cataloguing in Publication Data.
A catalogue record of this book is available
From the British |Library

First Published in 2015
by
For The Right Reasons
(Charity no. SCO37781)
Printer and Publishers
60 Grant St, Inverness
Tel 01463 718844 or 07717457247
fortherightreasons@rocketmail.com

It was his idea to launch Highland Homeless at Christmas and his idea to acquire the premises which remain a homeless shelter in Inverness city centre. His idea, too, to launch a Food for Families to provide hot meals for needy people each winter has become so popular that prisoners at Inverness Prison now cook for it. As well as chairing the committee, David and his wife Anne donate substantial amounts of mince each winter.

In business, he doesn't mince his words, but in charity he's come up with a mince mountain!

He was chairman at the launch of the Highland Archie Appeal, to which he donated £150,000, and he steered the appeal to raise £1 million in 15 months for a state of the art children's ward for Raigmore Hospital, Inverness.

He was an original guarantor at the launch of what is now Inverness Caledonian Thistle FC, and when he later took over as chairman he was astute enough to remove a £4 million debt which seemed to leave the club months to live. When two new stands were required in 60 days to meet the criteria for Premier League entry, he organised it.

Regularly at functions, the auction features prizes donated by David, who has become a 'go to' donor for fundraisers.

Little wonder that when he received his CBE, it was for services to charity as well as the construction industry.

His wife Anne and daughters Caroline and Tina are always close to his heart and he enjoys spending time with them in rural retreats in Argyll and Sutherland.

I spoke at his 50th birthday bash and again at his 60th and as the decades tumbled, I've got to know a warm-hearted character, occasionally blunt speaking but always ready with a laugh or an anecdote. In recent years, the arrival of five grandchildren has brought out a side in David you might not have anticipated.

He'll do a deal for a six figure sum by phone then set it down to continue to babysit his grandchild......

However much he indicates that he is running down his activities, I suspect there are more intriguing chapters yet to be penned in the David Sutherland story.

INDEX

1. INTRODUCTION

I set out to write a short history of Tulloch. The more I thought about it the more I realised that I've spent thirty years plus of my life contributing to the Tulloch journey so what follows is my perception of the route we chose, the terrain we encountered, the scenery we observed, the diversions we took, and how they all panned out ensuring that, as a whole, *'We've Come A Long Way'*, both corporately and personally.

Tulloch was a small, provincial, locally creative company born in Nairn in 1925. It had international ambition and a staggering growth strategy that was implemented in force, particularly in the 70s through to 90s. It propelled into being one of Scotland's top construction companies, and was very successful on the UK stage for a great number of years.

A great deal of recognition is due to every member of staff employed who were all integral to the journey and steadfastly stood by us through the good and the bad with support from the Royal Bank of Scotland, Clydesdale Bank and Dunfermline Building Society. From the mid 90s through to the turbulent times which emerged in 2008 the Bank of Scotland and their teams were most supportive and aligned on the journey. Sadly, following upon the Lloyds

TSB takeover of HBOS in Autumn 2008, matters became tortuous and frankly difficult.

We all understand that people have a job to do but forces were at work here to remove "old guards" throughout many corporate vehicles within the HBoS portfolio, presumably because you had linkages to senior HBoS management and I am sure many individuals are reviewing their records in light of current developments on the attitude and actions of certain banks in the sector.

Bank of Scotland strapline for many years was *a friend for life* – Hmmm maybe not so post 2008! But hey ho everybody had a job to do and I had a great respect for the BOS team.

Like any business we've had our critics, and like any good business we've had staunch supporters. Edinburgh based Robert Smith had the gumption to invest in Tulloch in the late 80s after recognising that it was a company waiting to burst into action. Our thanks to Robert, who is now Lord Smith of Kelvin, is important. He was instrumental in giving us support, providing a backbone and the vision to grow the business, and creating meaningful value. Ably assisted by Norman Murray he helped us to take our place on the national stage. Gavin Masterton, who rose through the ranks to become Treasurer and Managing Director of the Bank of Scotland and Ian Robertson, (now sadly deceased), an MD of the corporate division were immensely influential, particularly in the dramatic days when we saw rocketing growth, as was our principal customer over the decades, Kevin McCabe of Scarborough Property Group Plc. Kevin was a local Sheffield lad who had moved to Scarborough but built a huge property empire over the years spanning the globe, America, Canada, China, Australia, Singapore – you name it and Kevin was there.

Four of the five Tulloch brothers are now deceased. We owe them gratitude and respect for the early days when they laid the solid foundations of the business.

Thank you to everyone who has played a role in the development of the company through dedication, loyalty, commitment, expertise and professionalism. My particular thanks go to the old management team who enabled Tulloch to retain strength and vision irrespective of the turbulent business economy – George Fraser, Kenny Cameron, Neil Cameron, Donald Mackenzie, Charlie Monks and many more home grown Tulloch people who grew up into top roles in the Tulloch business over the years.

People make a business. People hold a business together. People make a business strong and reliable. I dedicate this book to the late David Philip and Sandy Tulloch. David was my much respected partner in the early years. Sandy, as our Life President (sadly now deceased) gave me unwavering support from 1979 onwards.

The Tulloch journey transcended many eras, pre war, post war, the 50s and 60s and the first real milestone was the construction of the oil yards at Ardersier and Nigg kicking off a great deal of economic activity for a company, all the individuals involved and the economy of the Highlands in general.

Politically we straddled periods of Conservative and Labour rule notwithstanding that we had mainly Liberal Democrat MPs and this brought us into contact with people like George Younger, Russell Johnston, Ian Lang and John Major (I always had a regret that I never met the Iron Lady Margaret Thatcher).

The Labour team was pretty formidable in these days and I remember clearly the Harold Wilson era and a very stern Willie Ross as Scottish Secretary of State.

As we progressed through the years David Stewart, a local boy, became our MP working at Westminster, and David was excellent in supporting not only the Highlands and Islands and Inverness in particular but also Inverness Caledonian Thistle FC and he never failed to mention Caley Thistle in his speeches in the House of Commons. He invited Roy Fox, the Managing Director of Scottish Provincial Press, and myself down to meet Tony Blair at 10 Downing Street one evening. Roy and I have vowed never to drink in the House of Commons 'Strangers' Bar again, and whilst we remembered our trip to Downing Street we particularly remember more the headache the next morning. We met some pretty stunning people, Tony Blair first of all who we were introduced to personally, John Reid, David Blunkett, Caroline Flint and many many more including DB's dog. However, we didn't meet Gordon Brown on the Downing Street trip but then when you read all the memoirs, he was Persona Non Grata in the Blair social circles.

We did meet Gordon Brown when he was Chancellor, never as PM. He was invited to open our apprentice training academy in 2004 in Inverness and we were asked to assemble outside the academy with 50 or 60 apprentices surrounding me as Chairman to welcome the Chancellor. Out of his car he bounded – he was a big guy – up he strolled and shook my hand "How did you know it was me who was hosting?" I asked. This was teeing him up for a joke, as I was about to explain that I was the oldest apprentice on the block, but he didn't stir me "I have a photograph" he retorted!

We proceeded to open the academy, he was very good with the young people who worked there and he gave us great encouragement that training was the way forward. The economy was great and Labour were in recess fighting and winning the election for a second term.

Gordon Brown got a lot of the credit for that era of prosperity and growth.

2. PERSONAL PATH

A three bedroomed council house in the Hilton area of Inverness from 1951 was home to my five younger siblings and me. My Gran, Margaret Simpson (née Fraser) also lived with us; she was pivotal to our personal development and growth, dishing out praise and discipline in equal measure. She was our anchor and housekeeper, ensuring retribution if we strayed off the straight and narrow. Both my parents worked tirelessly to make ends meet and bring up a family of six in a working class environment.

DFS at three years old with Granny Margaret

It's been said that my Gran saw me as a substitute for her son, Sandy, (my mother's brother) who died young from a measles infection in 1927; perhaps that is why she was determined to help me become successful. I wanted for nothing as a child; if my friend received a new bicycle my Gran, who also worked as a general housekeeper, would magically produce one. She worked hard and saved!

My upbringing was modest. Our home provided only three bedrooms, one bathroom and a lounge that seated five; my family totalled nine. My siblings; Lydia, John, Charles, Derek and George were all born in quick succession after me in 1949. We were big supporters of the Church of Scotland (in the evolution of the new Hilton Church), and regularly attended Sunday School, Boys Brigade, Cubs and Scouts, or Brownies and Guides. We were brought up with strong principles and morals.

My sister became a children's nurse, and each time one of my brothers turned 15 my father, a British Rail locomotive engineer (train driver to most!), insisted that they earn a living and steered them towards the British Army in the rank and file.

John and Derek thrived in this environment and had very successful careers, but Charles and George had many disputes on strategic matters with the military leadership. They left the army (Charles earlier than George) opting for the good life on civvy street.

As a family our motto is 'never forget your roots'. I think everybody today remembers where we came from and how hard it was for our folks.

My parents, as members of the working class, always voted Labour. My Gran was fiercely opposed, in particular, to Harold Wilson, and would regularly sit in front of the television audibly debating with him as he spoke to the nation. I have no doubt that some of my 'political spin' has come from listening to such rhetoric. My grandmother suffered from dementia and died in 1985 in Craig Dunain, Inverness. In these days the Health Board strategy for this debilitating disease failed to recognise the requirement for dignity, as Craig Dunain was a psychiatric institution and I always thought that dementia should be treated within another environment. Care, however, was first class.

My Gran, mum and dad all strived to bring three wages into the house so we were fed, watered and clothed. My Gran encouraged my education, supporting me through my years initially at the Highland Orphanage School, followed by Crown, then Hilton Primary School and Inverness Royal Academy (1961-1967).

My school days were lazy and mischievous and I seemed to be permanently at war with the authorities and the then rector of Inverness Royal Academy, W F MacDonald, or 'Fatlips' (now deceased) to his friends. I didn't count myself as a friend! My general lethargy and lack of discipline became even more evident when I secured only two highers in my final school years. I was determined to be an RAF pilot and my exam results were just enough to get me in. I also had hay fever to contend with but had never given this a moment's thought in terms of how it might affect me as a pilot. At a debrief at RAF Biggin Hill I was asked what I planned to do if I didn't get in; I confidently told the briefing officer that I would join one of the professions. I don't think I even really understood what a 'profession' was, but it seemed like an appropriate answer. Hay fever and not being good with a joystick put paid to my chosen route for a career!

The only contact I had with a profession was that the gentleman my grandmother kept house for was a Chartered Accountant (Mr R A MacWilliam), and on my visits to his home I noted the affluence and high standard of living. I wanted the same. What did a Chartered Accountant do? I didn't really know but it somehow became my career. I left Inverness Royal Academy in 1967 and became a trainee Chartered Accountant (CA) at the princely sum of £250 per year with John C Frame and Company (York House, 20 Church Street, Inverness). It was a small partnership led by Jack Frame. He also had many other business interests and was ably supported by Harry Brown and Jimmy Pringle. I fell under the tutelage of Harry and another employee, Donnie McLucas. It was a solid and beneficial initiation into the real business world. At this time I also enjoyed the company of a girlfriend who's father was also a chartered accountant, living in a large house of the Crown area of Inverness, so I began to associate this profession with 'comfort and good living' if you worked hard.

I knew from my upbringing that working hard was the key to success. When he wasn't driving trains my father would repair bicycles in a sweat shop on Castle Street (now Café 1), and tended private gardens. His efforts to support his family (not to mention his forty a day cigarette habit) were relentless.

Even in my early days at John C Frame and Company the desire to further myself was emerging as I trudged the dreary path into the CA Apprenticeship. I struck up an unofficial partnership with a young man, Frank Blincow (now deceased), and we executed book keeping 'homers.' Technically the use of the word 'homer' is questionable as we did the work in the office when our trusting bosses thought we were studying. It was a nice little earner, though I suspect it wouldn't be permissible these days! Entrepreneurial or what – it didn't make any money really!

As part of my studies I attended a one year non grad course at Glasgow University which incorporated aspects of law, accounting and economics.

I have a vague recollection of leaving Inverness one autumn afternoon with no idea where I was going to stay when I reached the big city. A trip to the university accommodation office led me to a basement bedsit at 26 Park Circus, a splendid Victorian circle of houses overlooking Kelvingrove Park. The house was owned by a disabled lady, Mrs Duvoisin, who rented out rooms to schoolteachers, young professionals and students. I shared a kitchen and bathroom with two other guys; compared to my cramped home in Hilton it was huge and what a treat to have my own room!

I created a new social life in Glasgow and quickly became a regular visitor to the Students' Union and the bars around Byres Road. It didn't take me long to suss out that the nurses at the Western Infirmary were a good source of social interaction, and it was on one of these trips to the Highlanders Institute on Barclay Street (beside Charing Cross) that I met my wife Anne (1970). I think it was the last dance! Anne was a trainee nurse at the Western Infirmary, and latterly a trainee midwife at the Queen Mother's Hospital. We never forget the Highlanders Institute – it probably did its job!

We tied the knot two years later, in 1972, in Glendaruel, on the Cowal Peninsula, where Anne's father owned a dairy farm. Their work ethic mirrored my own, and even if only visiting for a weekend you had to feed or milk the cows, then bottle and deliver it. In winter Anne and I had the

11

choice of putting £4 in our gas meter or spending £1.50 each on the bus to Argyll; hot food and family team work won on many occasions.

Anne and I had our first owned home on Byres Road in Glasgow, 141 to be precise! She bought it. If you're a pub expert you might like to know that we were above the Avalon pub, opposite the Rubaiyat, and three minutes from the changing rooms at the Western Infirmary! On the same street we had Curlers and Tennents, and a very trendy bar not far away on Hyndland Road, called The Rock. They're all still there! The flat was purchased from a colleague of Anne's at the Western Infirmary who was emigrating to Australia so we purchased it lock stock and barrel and we still have furniture and pieces from there to this day.

We had planned to return to Inverness after we married but instead I chose to work for an associated firm in Glasgow, Kerr McLeod and MacFarlan through a route that Donnie McLucas had taken when he'd been completing his training. We really enjoyed Glasgow as a city and it was handy for the trips to Glendaruel, particularly in winter time.

However in some ways in my years as a trainee I was probably leaning towards a rebel where I regarded study as a chore, and at this early stage my tolerance of anything was haphazard in a strange way.

However I kept telling myself to knuckle down and I probably concluded that getting married was a very positive move as it took some of the anger and rebellious streak out me. Turning up for DIETS of CA exams without studying was frankly stupid and it took a year or so for the penny to drop!

I also recall my stint as an air cadet when my hair was long – not a good idea in military circles and another example of my incorrect attitude!

3. RETURN TO THE HIGHLANDS

A property spurt in Glasgow prompted us to sell, and, having doubled our (her!) money, we moved back to Inverness. I joined MacWilliam Smith; the connection was none other than R A MacWilliam for whom my grandmother had worked, and where my appetite for the finer things in life had begun all those years ago.

Office politics and the usual rigmarole made me unsettled. I spotted and pursued a niche role; following a local government reorganisation in 1975 lots of local authorities were failing to tidy up the previous authority's accounts. I made myself available to carry out a management service which involved preparing (very boring!) Abstracts of Accounts. It was a really tricky situation given that they were Cessation Abstracts with balances transferring to new authorities. I reported to a single partner, but really I was my own boss for a couple of years.

Experience and a good network of contacts meant that I had picked up some mainstream audits for the new district councils, and I was, for a while, interacting with the Council's Director of Finance on Skye. He offered me a job as Depute Director of Finance. It sounded like a great opportunity. However, I was in the latter stages of my CA exams which meant that if I didn't pass I would be condemned to becoming an audit clerical assistant! This held less than zero appeal. The added bonus of a subsidised mortgage and a cheap car loan reeled me in as Anne and I were now also proud parents to Caroline by this stage in 1975. We hedged our bets!

Life on Skye may sound idyllic but winter was bitter and I sat there preparing Abstracts of Accounts so that my boss, the then Director, could travel the length and breadth of Britain, ramp up his expenses, and attend numerous conferences. For what? I still don't know the answer.

My role also involved supervising the Accounts Department. It was here that I learned the most about accountability for the public purse. As luck would have it I sat my finals in the spring (when I moved to Skye I did not know if I would pass or fail). My father phoned in August to tell me I'd passed. Let's call it sod's law!

After all I had re-sat up to two exams on a five year roll – that in today's analysis is a waste of 2 years!

However dogged determination and focus got me through and I passed. It wasn't needed, this very difficult course necessitating working long into the night. Needless to say the last lap was a cramming exercise and it worked.

My salary of £250 a year as an apprentice, in the beginning, didn't impress my father. That said, he offered to frame my ICAS certificate. His suggestion said it all; I had recognition from my Pop. My mother and my gran were also immensely proud of my achievement. At the District Council I earned a princely £7,500 per annum!

My repetitive district council work became a chore so I redirected myself to another challenge by taking on a financial controller's position with a Skye based contractor. This became rather a tricky assignment when the incumbent finance director moved to Canada. What was even trickier was that I couldn't work out why he was going!

However, I soon found out. It turned out that a civil engineering job being carried out at Strollamus, on the Broadford to Portree road, had started to show losses. My colleagues and directors scoffed at my revelation and assured me that I was wrong. I had made no mistake. There was a geological problem, a kettle hole in the line of the road, (subsea) and all of the fill being put onto site was being sucked into this gap. Of course, it was not being measured by the surveyors and didn't produce the vital cashflow!

The directors thought that they could 'claim' for this event; they could not. Instead they instigated a bank refinancing of the business which I assisted with. At the end of the process they gathered the Management Team and asked if we would inject money into the business. Many of the team agreed but I declined, as part of the request involved the granting of a personal guarantee and I didn't want to put my family at risk. On that basis, I was sacked. I had a wife and young daughter to support.

The previous week I had sent Anne and Caroline back to the mainland on holiday but the Directors now informed me that I could use my company car only as far as Kyleakin; I had to take the ferry to Kyle as a passenger, and catch the train to Inverness. What a time for reflection this turned out to be! The world had taught me a harsh lesson and forced me to grow up. My initial bitterness about the experience soon dissipated and hindsight tells me that my decision was right; the firm went bust two years later.

4. HIGHLANDS AND ISLANDS DEVELOPMENT BOARD AND THE TRANSITION TO TULLOCH

My move back to Inverness made the Highlands and Islands Development Board (HIDB) my next port of call thanks to Bill Whyte who worked for HIDB. Bill actually worked with me to provide support (grant assistance) on a quarrying operation we had opened up at Sconser through the Skye based civil engineering business I worked for. It was later acquired by Tulloch which showed that I bore no grudges, and I am still friends with the two brothers who originally owned the business and indeed they carried out construction work on a property we owned in Skye.

When I joined HIDB it had a remit to generate and sustain economic development throughout the territory. Whilst as an organisation it was often wrongly maligned, I felt that it was an excellent platform that enabled exposure to a whole range of different types of business. This was a fantastic insight into business issues in remote locations.

Perhaps one of my more memorable and 'spectacular' cases at HIDB was the sale of a Thurso based contracting company to an Orkney contractor who was seeking to expand his empire to the mainland. Neither party realised that when I first completed the case (it was fast-tracked) I had recommended to the Board that we reject it. However, the then Deputy Chairman of HIDB, David Dunbar-Naismith, advised me to 'make the deal happen', and since he was a retired Rear Admiral I decided his words must be wise. We went back to the drawing board and found a viable way for the merger. The two businesses traded well together for a number of years; the Orkney principals are now retired or deceased. Being a creative creature of habit, Tulloch subcontracted business to the Thurso firm, even as recently as 2009.

Sir Kenneth Alexander was the Chairman of the HIDB and I worked alongside him on a very innovative press printing system that involved facsimile printing of the Daily Star and Express in Inverness. We were soon up against elements of the Trade Unions (NGA and Sogat) who blocked the opening, and boycotted the position. As a result the HIDB lost significant money.

I had recommended that we agree this initiative but I'd also stipulated that union agreement was imperative. A 'waiver' process meant that my boss at HIDB signed off the transaction whilst ignoring my recommendation on the union. It was a decision that clearly came back to bite him.

During this period I brushed against many powerful Trade Unionists like Brenda Dean, Bill Keys, Jocelyn Stevens (Managing Director of Express Newspapers), and an individual from Trafalgar House PLC named Victor Matthews, who was one of Britain's leading businessmen. What can I say? A 'young green horn' from Inverness going to talk to these guys was like a goldfish visiting *Sea World* and swimming with killer sharks!

In these days I also worked with a number of professional firms, but Frame Kennedy and Forrest (Inverness) headed by Harry Brown and Andrew Duncan received the bulk of my assignments on the grounds that I knew them well. Their professional capacity to deliver projects was renowned and their professional opinion much valued.

I have many fond memories of my time at HIDB and I see it as a thoroughly fruitful experience. There are many people I have helped who I will always remember, but of course, having signed the Official Secrets Act I cannot mention them by name!

There is, of course, one exception to every rule; Jim Cowie received some assistance from HIDB to open a fish factory in Wick creating numerous employment opportunities.

Jim approached us with an abundance of enthusiasm and we concluded business negotiations with him, and his wife Mary, in their home in Wick. To this day Jim is a successful businessman in Caithness, and he owns an award winning restaurant in Scrabster, Captain's Galley and has remained a friend.

Time to move on!

My HIDB connections meant that Harry Brown and Andrew Duncan engineered four interviews to persuade me to join Tulloch as Financial Controller. It was really due to my respect for Harry and Andrew that I agreed to the interview process at all. I vividly remember meeting the five Tulloch brothers in a room at Corrie Lodge (Milburn Road, Inverness) akin to a television shot of how the Arabian Kings met visitors in the Middle East, except that this time they were in cloth caps instead of robes! They put their very best efforts into convincing me that this was a superb job and that they took on board all advice that their financial advisors offered; did they hell?!

Tina was born in May 1978 so there was added incentive to try to get it right in terms of the main family provider but Anne also deserves credit as she returned to her profession as a midwife at Raigmore Hospital in between giving birth to the children.

Finally, in December 1979 I took the plunge and accepted the position with Tulloch having decided within myself that I wasn't a very good accountant and, given my experiences with HIDB, I knew that I felt more comfortable working in a business environment. For the avoidance of all doubt I now repeat that I had more of an eye for the business opportunity than for accountancy.

It was an interesting transition. The company was disorganised; the brothers bickered regularly. They were insular, secretive, and they made no attempt to manage the business as a group (which it clearly was).

However, I appeared to fit in instantly, and adhered to my strong work ethic. I can still hear my late mother in law lamenting: "David, what sort of a job is it that you have?! You're working long hours, travelling away from home, spending Saturdays in the office!" Let me tell you now, it was pure dedication as I look back.

5. EARLY DAYS OF TULLOCH AND INTERNATIONAL PURSUITS

Tulloch started as a small joinery business in Nairn in 1925, and, akin to many businesses of the time, it augmented joinery work with 'undertaking' (on an ad hoc basis). Working as undertakers kept the joiners busy when there was no on-site work, and what a platform undertaking turned out to be for Alexander (Sandy) Tulloch! He was busy plying his wares around Nairn, burying the great and the good, and having a whale of a time organising, attending funerals, and enjoying regular drams to toast the dead. Johnnie Walker Black Label was the favourite tipple!

The Tulloch family at that time comprised five brothers and two sisters who were marshalled by Alexander Tulloch (senior) and Mrs Tulloch. They operated from a small house, Ruthven, just outside Nairn.

Alexander Tulloch (senior) was passionate about his family and created elasticity within his small business empire to accommodate his sons as they came of age. John and Sandy Tulloch worked alongside their father, whilst Willie and Kenny initially ran the plant and haulage side of the business. Donald was dedicated to the plant hire and civil engineering business. Timber processing was allocated to Willie. The building side of the company was added at a later date, potentially when the business grew and was carrying out regular work for the estates and landed gentry around the Highlands (early clients included the Whitbread family in Kinlochewe).

From their Ruthven base the family expanded the business to take on Nairn offices in Rose Street, Acre Street and High Street. Some of these office premises were sold in the 1990s. The business acquired 86-88 High Street, which was formerly the British Linen Bank; the family took great pride in trumpeting that they had bought the bank! Technically, of course, it was true.

Alexander Tulloch (senior) died in 1963 having established solid business roots for his sons.

However, the business, like many, had its ups and downs, and the odd overseas issue to contend with. From a Tulloch perspective, the biggest breakthrough was when the oil construction yard at Ardersier was mooted. I don't think it was any great secret at the time, but George Wimpey, via their George MacWilliam subsidiary, put in one of the lowest bids. Unfortunately for them, the American rule was never to trust the lowest price and instead used it to negotiate with the other bidders. The Tulloch family managed to convince the American management that they had the skill, drive, enthusiasm and technical know-how to build the yard to their specification. It was one of the largest jobs in the Highlands at the time, and this was the defining moment when the business was transformed from a small

Nairnshire firm to a significant player in the North of Scotland.

Prior to the McDermott initiative Donald Tulloch had relocated his family to South Africa where he'd set up a Tulloch venture outside Johannesburg focussing on the petrochemical industry. The Tulloch family decided that Donald's skills were urgently required for the McDermott job and lured him back. As a result the South African business was wound down, and the Ardersier job made a great name for itself, the Tulloch name being firmly stamped on it.

The Americans always found new work for Tulloch on the yard, allowing it to lend expertise to facilities' management where it utilised the building, plumbing, electrical and ancillary services, right through to a permanent Cat grader being on site to take care of any potholes. As the water tables in the Ardersier yard moved up and down, 'cost plus' was the norm, and very profitable. The haulage, building, and civil engineering business was also utilised at the yard for many years.

Many other businesses in the Highlands, such as the MacWilliam company (then part of Wimpey), Balfours (then based in the Highlands), Amec, and indeed our old friends at Morrison Construction, were all, understandably, envious of the Tulloch relationship with Ardersier.

Between South Africa and Ardersier, Donald Tulloch's drive for international business led him to Saudi Arabia in a joint venture, Famco Tulloch, with a Saudi Prince as a partner (this was required by Saudi law). It quickly turned out to be problematic, and a cash guzzler. The general company activity in Saudi involved a series of concrete batching plants in Eastern Province; to the untrained mind that most likely smacks of 'taking coals to Newcastle'. Donald subsequently ran into health problems and was hospitalised in the UK. The Saudi venture fell apart. The partner did not live up to expectation, and a strategy was devised to withdraw.

The mastermind of this strategy was Harry Brown, a friend of the Tulloch family and my first boss. Harry, and Sandy Tulloch, were sent out on mission 'damage limitation' and, having tried, somewhat unsuccessfully, to wrap it all up, emerged from Saudi Arabia on a dhow (sailing vessel usually used to carry heavy trading items) to connect with their flight home! Clearly Sandy Tulloch didn't fancy 50 lashes. I still maintain that he was the 'wrong person' to extract us from a toxic venture in a foreign land! Nevertheless, he flew back to the UK on his birthday and celebrated with a dram of his beloved Black Label, with Harry a much relieved man sitting beside him.

Tulloch continued to prosper bringing in business units with Boyd and Martin, and Donald Davidson Plumbing and

Heating; these fell under the control of the building divisions and, in my opinion, were not well managed at that time!

Quarrying also emerged with some sand and gravel deposits on the River Nairn, which led to developing a relationship with Cawdor and Moray estates. A contract 'crushing division' flourished from this activity 'gypsy style' as teams of crusher equipment and loading shovels set about crushing rock on the paths of new roads and motorways. They provided an alternative to cash intensive capital expenditure for road builders by working as quarrying operatives in their own right. We funded everything on Hire Purchase but carefully linked it to cashflow from the contracts.

As these units were added for solid commercial reasons, it meant that the Tulloch offering was almost a one-stop-shop by the 80s. A multi faceted organisation was exactly what the Highlands needed after the boom years of the Hydro expansions in the 1960s, and the creation of the two oil yards.

Whilst most of the opportunities outside the Ardersier contract were focused on tender (for example, the roads), we also carried out sub-contracts for large companies (Tractor Shovels, Amec, Glasgow based Whatlings). Tulloch, one way or another, got involved in most stretches of the then new A9 construction. I often look back in awe at that business era and wonder how it happened.

When I first joined Tulloch, we had in-house accountants who worked in smoke filled rooms in Inverness and Nairn. I was initially based in Nairn but quickly moved to the Corrie Lodge office in Inverness where I could feel the real buzz. Corrie Lodge has formed a big part of my life, and today one of the family businesses has a material interest in the building which operates as a business centre and has a portrait of the Tulloch founder, Alexander Tulloch Senior, in the Boardroom!

6. CHALLENGES GALORE

Life in Tulloch, in the early days, was nothing short of a monumental challenge. I was regularly faced with the aftermath of the out of control Famco Tulloch (the failed Saudi business venture). Although most of it was dealt with in the two years before I joined Tulloch, the legacy that it left was a real poison pill in the form of financial debt. The currency exchange also worked against us.

Our bankers at the time, Bank of Scotland, became very nervous, and, although the family kept that quiet, I don't make a great secret of it. I was parachuted into the administrative headquarters of the Bank of Scotland in the Grassmarket, Edinburgh with Harry Brown on at least one or two occasions. It's fair to say that the Tulloch family's forte was not 'liaising' with bankers. The bulk of the work fell to Harry, and was then inherited by me.

Matters were further complicated by a construction job at Bank of Scotland, 9 High Street, Inverness, that went horrendously off the rails. Hindsight tells me that the problem did not belong to the Bank, but resided firmly within our contract management system and in particular, one family member who may have interfered with the job a little too much. At that time David Philip was the (somewhat exasperated) building manager, and we became good friends and colleagues. One morning Sandy Tulloch informed me that a notice had gone up on site saying the contract had 'been determined.' The gates were locked. The Bank of Scotland had actually thrown us off the job! It was a horrific situation if you bear in mind that at this time we were in tentative discussions about how we were going to sort out the Saudi debacle. Now we were in the midst of a contractual crisis with the very funder which called the shots!

Rising through the ranks at the bank was Gavin Masterton. He asked us what our strategy was to extricate ourselves from the Saudi saga. We told him we were intent on lowering the debt by increasing our construction activity on a cash positive basis (augmented by diversifying our spread of business units).

Thankfully, the Bank of Scotland had the guts and the vision to back us, and at that juncture an obvious opportunity arose for us in the form of Corrie Industrial Services Limited, a company that supplied manpower to the McDermott yard at Ardersier. Under our management we took the company all over the world and were pioneers in places like Kazakhstan and Vietnam. We terminated our connection with this business at the turn of the century when we decided to concentrate more on core activities.

There have been many changes in the company structure and the nature of the business since 1925, but throughout it all we've acknowledged Alexander Tulloch (senior), the boss. We have a portrait of him in all our UK offices including Corrie Lodge which was a base for, would you believe it, Corrie Recruitment Limited, a 2012 version of Corrie Industrial Services Limited in the 90s

I believe that it's important never to forget your roots, so I herald that the Tulloch empire was born in Nairn, and that the individual with the vision to put together a multi-faceted business was Alexander Tulloch (senior), the 'boss' as he was affectionately known. Congratulations Tulloch on reaching the grand old age of 90 in 2015. Also without JV Interaction we would not have achieved our ambitions and I pay tribute to our partners:

Bank of Scotland
British Linen Bank
County Properties
Scarborough Properties
Peter Fowler/Roy Fox
Upland developments Aviemore
David Cameron/Alan Munro
Teesland Group
M&K Macleod Lochgilphead
Stephen Brazier London
Whatlings PLC Glasgow
Scott & Les from Aberdeen
Bond Manpower from Melbourne (Rose & Yana)
Grant Sword
Muir Mackay

7. THE TIDE TURNS AND THE ASSOCIATED TURBULENT WATERS

Great stories abound about the Tulloch connection at Nairn and how we went about our business. One of the encounters that I remember most fondly is the construction and development of a lodge for Madame De Rochambeau who was very connected in French high society. It was only accessible through a ford on a river high in the hills of Moray. But, Madame, being a generous individual, insisted on throwing a party for our team even though the job completed late! The final scenes were akin to a military retreat; it seems that our men took to the very fine tasting French wine with great gusto, and clearly paid the penalty as they retreated to Nairn across the river ford as drunk as skunks!

Tulloch was undergoing a period of transformation and was surrounded by individuals who were pivotal in influencing the direction of the business. We branched out from Nairn to Inverness and then became national. David Philip, Ronnie Fraser, George Fraser, Neil Cameron, Kevin Bisset, Kenny Cameron, and Gerry Job are a few of the key players; the list is long!

When I joined Tulloch one of my first tasks was to reorganise five individual companies owned by five brothers into one group; in very simple terms we had a building company that was losing a fortune, a civil engineering company that was making a fortune, and 'developing' businesses in the quarry, plant, transport man power and timber industries that were guzzling capital.

A Tulloch and Sons (Holdings) Ltd was formed, and started to bring people forward, including David Philip and myself. Although it was hard to break into the family bastion of the holding company we nevertheless started to see the more senior members of the new team, such as David and me, taking on directorships. It was the first break in family tradition. Ronnie Fraser, who was our civil engineering director, also became a company director. He chose to seek pastures new in the 90s.

David Philip had the unenviable task of bringing the building company into line and generating profit. We quickly realised that by being judicious with our contract management we could generate cash upfront to help fund the growing, cash guzzling, parts of the business – the maxim of cash being king featured as part of our vocabulary.

As a humble accountant with big drive and ambition, and supported by Donald and Ken Tulloch, I was motivated to create cash and repay the Tulloch Saudi debts quickly. We were soon cash positive. We had an idea to merge our successful trading business with a large mass of land on the Cromarty Firth, known as Highland Deephaven, and owned by an offshoot of the Brown-Root family (famous in the oil business in the States around Houston).

Using our expertise we believed that we could bring development opportunities for their land (once again we noticed the word 'development' had popped up in the Tulloch portfolio). We thought we could buy tranches of land and turn them into topside activities that would generate profit for us, and as a by-product generate work for our construction company. The main brief was not to tie up valuable capital or cash.

The Highland Deephaven experience was excellent. We appointed a 'broker', Robert Smith, who was the Managing Director of National Commercial and Glynns (an offshoot of the Royal Bank of Scotland). He was acting as an advisor for both sides. A man of stature, Alexander MacMillan, the then General Manager of the Clydesdale Bank and a director of Highland Deephaven, acted on behalf of the Brown-Root family, and we set sail to make this deal work.

The Deephaven merger did not occur, but our relationship with the team was strong, particularly through Bob Kirkpatrick, their locally based MD. Whilst we dismounted the corporate deal, we executed the very type of transaction we craved; we built the spooling jetty for the then Apache Barge at Deephaven, at vast risk to our company, but also accruing vast profit. The structure still proudly protrudes into the Cromarty Firth, and has withstood the test of time and weather and still spools pipelines onto barges and is now operated by a huge French company called Technip. I didn't see a Tulloch in the office for 6 months while this job was underway – heaven!

Novar Estate was pivotal to the process; we rented a rock and sand and gravel quarry from them. We chose not to develop the rock quarry, and instead opted to move to another quarry at Strathrory, saving the cost of opening up the negotiated Novar position.

By this point we had a range of businesses, and the Highland Deephaven experience brought a continuing relationship with Robert Smith, to the extent that when one of the Tulloch brothers was signalled as being an exit candidate (John Tulloch), Robert and his team, Norman Murray (former Chair of Cairn Energy and more recently, Chair of Petrofac Plc), agreed to acquire 20% of Tulloch from John for what I can best describe as a 'not insubstantial' sum. Robert preferred not to take a seat on the Board and left us to our own devices.

Robert brought the power needed to reorganise the group effectively and introduced the word 'stewardship', which the family hated to hear. Everything was battened down to ensure that we were a technically, and administratively, professional company. Once the group was reorganised, the family announced that it was time to retire (approximately 1983). At this time 'retiring' meant selling the business; this led to the second break in tradition.

I raised the issue of sweat equity; I'd spent long hours reorganising the group with Harry Brown, and agonising over how best to diversify. During this time the construction business completely changed and moved away from the traditional tendered markets to more negotiated markets. We developed a relationship with Kevin McCabe from County Properties Group and then The Scarborough Property Group. We undertook a job for Kevin converting a store on the corner of Inverness High Street and Inglis Street to Adams Clothing Company. The job went horribly wrong and ran over budget; we had a problem. The issue stemmed from the professional team where the architects were hesitant and the quantity surveyors didn't keep on top of the job. Generally speaking, there was a bit of a stramash.

We found the solution during a dinner with Kevin McCabe, his then assistant, Mike Burden (since deceased), and David Philip. We went to the Golf View Hotel in Nairn with the idea to thrash out the final account which was some £200,000 adrift. The meal was supervised by legendary hotelier Greta Anderson (also deceased), and involved several glasses of wine and then whisky (a lot of whisky).

Throughout the dinner Greta came through to pass me messages that Sandy Tulloch was on the phone. I accepted one call where he said: "We're not happy with you and David Philip handling this. We feel a family member should be there. I'll come now." The offer of help was robustly refused and we told him to leave us alone.

At the conclusion of the Kevin McCabe deal we were promised another transaction in the area to build a £3,000,000 supermarket if we conceded 50% of the final account; this would mean that our rock bottom expectation of receiving £100,000 was gambled on future activity.

I'm sure you can picture the scene the following morning in the Corrie Lodge amphitheatre, when David and I were called all sorts of idiots, fools, and met by protestations that we'd been conned and would never see work again. These were the polite comments! Interestingly, they didn't over-rule us!

This era was when I was effectively cutting my commercial teeth and taught me the importance of listening to your peers and to take on board other views. Harry Brown and Andrew Duncan were pivotal on the family business front. People like Robert Smith were very influential on the corporate stage from my perspective, and the person I learnt most from was Kevin McCabe who was and remained a very loyal customer first and foremost, but became a good friend to Tulloch Group and to me in particular as an individual.

A problem shared with Kevin more often than not had a very interesting twist I hadn't thought of with my take on it.

Now, picture the scene some six weeks later when we were awarded two supermarket building jobs on a negotiated building package basis. Our decision to gamble paid dividends to the extent that we carried out 47 negotiated jobs with that individual and his companies over the years. The payback was enormous, with Kevin benefitting via a relationship built on trust which delivered his projects within the feasibility parameters.

The family's wish to retire was the real turning of the tide. I decided to be bold at a new level and asked if I could buy some shares (given that the sweat equity was real). I was rejected with some very rude language which I understood communicated as 'go away young man' or something very similar.

Naturally, a conversation with Robert Smith representing the National Commercial and Glynn shareholders was held. I told him that I thought I could sell the company and the family could not sell it without my expertise. Well, this triggered quite a change of events; Robert agreed to sell me his shareholding at the princely sum of £679,000 for 20% of the equity.

I chose my moment carefully, when four of the Tulloch family members were present, and again asked to buy shares in the company. I was rebuffed once more, even less politely than before. I distinctly remember the word 'off' was somewhere in the sentence. I suggested that I buy the bank out. After a few moments they all stopped laughing and rolling around the room and agreed that I could buy the bank out. I knew they were all exchanging secret glances querying how I could possibly buy out the bank!

I bought the bank out. I went to Alex MacMillan who was still General Manager of the Clydesdale Bank – remember that name from the Highland Deephaven deal! He very simply asked what my strategy was. I told him the business was about to be put up for sale and I thought I could help sell it within six months and I explained that I had a number of contenders. He asked for the names. I rattled off, as you would, Tarmac, Balfour Beatty, Amec, and a company called Alfred McAlpine, all Plc's. Morrison couldn't afford us in those days!

To his eternal credit, Mr MacMillan agreed to enable me to complete the deal. There was a particularly poignant moment where he said: "Lad, do you realise that if this backfires you've lost everything?" I replied that I fully understood. I had borrowed £679,000. I lived with my family, Anne, Caroline and Tina in Lochardil in a house worth £10,000; our mortgage was £9,999. I quickly worked out that all that we would lose was the house, and self respect, but my conviction was that the business could be sold. I didn't share the risks involved with my wife Anne for several months!

At this juncture, Robert Smith, having sold his investment on behalf of National Commercial and Glynns Limited moved on but little did we guess that our paths would cross again in later years.

Donald Tulloch and I set about trying to convince people that we were a credible outfit that offered huge growth opportunity. We must also give credit to Whatlings Plc (Glasgow) who were part of the McAlpine empire, and also Tulloch joint venture partners.

Whatlings Plc were of the old school. Their Chairman, Cameron Lindsay, was a well respected industry member, and a recognised stock market stalwart in terms of his stewardship of that business. However, under the surface, Whatlings Plc, was changing, and a young guard began to emerge headed by Brian Fitzgerald (technical), and Rod Lawson (financial). It was exceptionally obvious to us that Rod was the finance director; when you walked into his office between 8.30am and 9am he was reading the Financial Times. We'd been on the go since 6.30am!!

The more we built our relationship with Rod and Brian the more it became clear that we could help them. Given that Tulloch had actually worked as subcontractors for a great number of years, the relationship with other team members was strong enough to thrust us forward, particularly as by this time Whatlings Plc were part of the Alfred McAlpine Group Plc so the match make opportunity was stark!

40

8. STILL WATERS RUN DEEP

Thanks to our earlier connections with Kevin McCabe, we had picked up other negotiated clients of stature, including Glass Glover Plc. It, in turn, was very well cemented into the then Presto, Safeway and Tesco distribution networks, and these networks necessitated huge sheds for storage of materials en route to supermarkets.

As a direct product of our marketing prowess, we picked up an order from Glass Glover for two huge sheds, one in Livingstone and one in Bathgate. The Bathgate shed was the largest one in Scotland at the time, but as I sat down in the Inverness office with David Philip we realised that we didn't have the expertise to build it! What a dilemma! We'd gone from having a £7-8million pounds turnover, to no resources to build it! We chose to partner with Whatlings Plc and Brian Fitzgerald and we set up Tulloch Whatlings Construction Limited as a 50/50 JV. My maxim was always that JVs gave us a share of something and halved the risk!

One of the contracts at Bathgate became an even more attractive proposition when John Bingham, the Managing Director of Glass Glover and his Development Director Peter Dicken, issued a challenge saying that if we finished the job by Christmas there would be a bonus of £120,000. If they could distribute from that location by December 1985 they would in turn win. We completed on time and scooped up the bonus. No-one believed we could earn it!

From here onwards each joint venture partner (Whatlings Plc and Tulloch Holdings) had substantial profit shares. I remember Brian Fitzgerald telling me of Owen Rich, the then Managing Director of Alfred McAlpine Plc, asking: "Who are these guys? How can they pick up this work?" Brian Fitzgerald relayed the connection, the history, and the fact that we had once tried to merge with Whatlings a number of years previously. From this, McAlpine developed a burning desire to acquire us in Scotland. Sadly Brian died very young of a heart attack in 2002, a much missed colleague, friend and respected character in our industry.

Remember that I had told Alex MacMillan that I could sell the business within six months? After a short period of gestation Alfred McAlpine became the preferred bidder. The company had a spread of activities that weren't too dissimilar to ours. After a long protracted negotiation we sold to them in 1987 for the princely sum of £5million, assisted greatly by the Whatlings connection.

Bear in mind that at this time I was a 20% shareholder; the deal we made was a modest sum of money upfront (which was the £5million), but we also had an 'earn out' mechanism over a two year period stating that if we grew the business, and earned profit, we could have a second payment. We did it, but vast quantities of water had gone under the bridge in the meantime.

McAlpine decided that the Tulloch business needed a Managing Director and Donald Tulloch was appointed as such, which was the first break in tradition within the family. Tulloch Holdings had previously worked on the basis that everybody had a view, and nobody voted. The logic was simple; if we didn't have a voting system we had to be certain that everybody agreed on the major decisions (and it stopped people saying 'I told you so' if anything went wrong). Shortly thereafter Donald also appeared in the McAlpine arena as the Deputy Chairman of the minerals division, and whilst we deserved our 'earn out', the road was riddled with challenges. However, I committed to a two year sojourn, and moved my family to Chester, as Finance Director of Alfred McAlpine Minerals Limited which had worldwide quarrying and related interests. My time with McAlpine was short, under 3 years.

9. ALFRED MCALPINE PLC – THE MBO AND POST THE MBO

The interim challenges at McAlpine Minerals were immense. We dealt with a series of acquisitions, and eventually disposals, and in between we had the usual gremlins, including one of the simplest abuses of management information I have ever witnessed!!

We had a business called Concrete Masonry Ltd that manufactured very lightweight building blocks (heklite blocks). The raw material was imported at vast expense from Iceland, and was processed from volcanic ash (how relevant these days). To make their figures look good, the management allegedly bulldozed mounds of earth and sprinkled heklite over it. Their surveyors dutifully came along, measured it as 'full-blown' heklite at vast cost, and hey presto, the accounts looked wonderful.

Regrettably, there was a similar management intervention at a Tulloch quarry outside Gourock when one of our colleagues decided to plot the size of a stockpile in relation to the quarry setting; this would certainly have put a blip on the Clyde landscape! The manager at the time was removed; the then directors back at old base should really have been held to account, instead they ran for the hills. At this time our relationship with McAlpine began to ebb. One of our operating executives had decided that influencing stock values and hence profits covered up many operational ills.

When drilled down this was a very embarrassing episode from a Tulloch viewpoint and, needless to say, the individual concerned moved on and the Tulloch team responsible for monitoring were, to say the least, pretty embarrassed and never really recovered from this. McAlpine, where I now worked, could have thrown the book at the Tulloch team for this episode but they stayed steadfastly loyal to us as we continued the journey and earned them some real tangible profits.

I wrote an eight page memo to our Chief Executive, Tony Scurr, explaining the Tulloch position on Gourock and Concrete Masonry, how this incident had occurred, and informing him what we were doing to remedy the situation. (I've kept a copy of this tome to this day – riveting reading!)

Two years into my sojourn at McAlpine's they began to hit worldwide cash problems, particularly in Africa. The business had a tremendous need to realise cash and quickly, given that it had been acquisitive over the previous five years, and at that stage was turning over £500m (a fairly significant amount in its time).

The Chairman, Bobby McAlpine, set up a Chairman's Disposal Committee of four or five people. I was representing the Minerals Division. The burning question was whether McAlpine would decide to keep Tulloch, or if there was more value in selling? I was in a difficult position as I was working professionally for McAlpine, and yet here we were discussing the future of Tulloch which was important to me, the Highlands, Scotland as a whole and all my old colleagues including David Philip as leader of the residual business in Inverness.

Obviously, sitting around this table at head office in Hooton on the Wirral in such august company, I decided to speak up to explain that these guys were former colleagues of mine, and that we should encourage the management team to consider a buy-out of the construction related business, minus the quarries. The conversation in the Tulloch team quickly concluded that a buy-out would only work if I returned to Inverness to help it. This created a new dilemma. I was content at McAlpine; I liked my job and the challenges it brought. It was in a different plane to the Scottish venture, but after some persuasion (particularly from David Philip), we decided to push ahead. A natural port of call for funding was Robert Smith, who was Head of Royal Bank Development Capital, but what we didn't realise was that he was about to move to Deutsche Bank.

The management buyout, by necessity, had to be fast tracked and came with interesting developments. I had travelled to Inverness with my family for a staff dance in December 1988 when I received a phone call from Euan McAlpine (my boss). He told me that he had good news and bad news. The good news was that I could keep the company plane for the weekend; the bad news was that because I was leading the management buyout I was sacked!

I understood clearly the conflict of interest issue which caused this, but felt that Euan and the McAlpine team hadn't understood the need for openness and honesty on both sides as, in effect, by engineering a management buyout, we were helping them via a cash injection of circa £5,000,000 to alleviate their cash problems, with them retaining the highly profitable Tulloch quarrying business within McAlpine.

I am glad to say that common sense ruled at the end of the day.

That aside it felt good, as an Inverness boy, to fly in the company plane into my hometown and whoop it up at a dance at what was then the Mercury Hotel.

A hurried gathering of the Tulloch team on the Saturday morning revealed that David Philip supported me to the hilt and threatened to resign if I was pushed out. I'm not so sure about the others, but they seemed to come round eventually. On returning to Chester, McAlpine's decision to sack me was reversed.

The deal was concluded, and the management buyout proceeded in February 1989. We paid £5m to repatriate the business (without the quarries) to Scottish ownership. This ownership was to differ from the previous family controlled model.

The family had shareholdings that were minor. David Philip, a few others and we took the lion's share, with Royal Bank Development Capital holding 41%.

We had significant assistance on the transaction from James McCormack (by then the legal director of McAlpine); this solid relationship was a real help.

Throughout the process of selling the business to McAlpine and buying it back again a young, thrusting, Glasgow lawyer, Ian Bankier, who worked for McGrigor Donald, appeared on the scene. He drove a hard bargain on our behalf, and limited our exposure to the various warranties that occur in these situations. Ian has remained a reliable advisor to the group; his input will always be remembered. A photograph of the Completion Meeting at Alfred McAlpine shows many faces; many of those individuals are no longer with us.

However, Tulloch was safely returned to Scottish hands, and our negotiated policy in the construction division motored on; we had a whole range of clients including supermarkets such as Safeways (they'd taken over Presto), Wm Low (now Tesco), and many others including Scottish Co-op.

The relationship with the Bank of Scotland had become stronger, notwithstanding that Royal Bank were the funders. Our relationship with Gavin Masterton also moved on a pace. We rapidly cemented the relationship with Bank of Scotland as our principal funder, notwithstanding that the Royal Bank was our equity player, but eventually we rationalised and used BOS as lead.

Following the management buyout we started life as an independent company during a recession. Our mainstream bankers were the Royal Bank of Scotland a the time, and our shareholders were Royal Bank Development Capital again (via our connection with Robert Smith). The lead however changed to Joe McGrane; his mission in life was to cash in. He started on a journey to sell the company before we had even really begun. He'd taken over the portfolio from Robert Smith and Norman Murray who had both moved to Morgan Grenfell Development Capital Ltd, a subsidiary of Deutsche Bank.

Life was tough, and even though we just about hit our targets each year and sales were mounting, our profits were stagnant because of the recession. We serviced our debt and held our own in torrid trading conditions.

As we settled down to business some future stars emerged from the woodwork; George Fraser was promoted to the board, and we had an excellent support team in the form of Bill MacLeod, Katherine Stewart, Kenny Cameron, Gerry Job, Neil Cameron, Donald Mackenzie and others. As time ticked on more and more of the family took a back seat. I think Willie Tulloch probably went to his grave criticising me for selling off the timber business which had previously seen us yo-yoing across a spectrum of raw material suppliers! Chile and Russia were also interfering with pricing! I decided it was better sold.

The timber business also needed significant capital investment, which we were not prepared to do. To progress matters we agreed a management buyout to Murray Gordon, who was a successful acquisition target of ours in the form of Perthshire Timber a number of years before. Willie Tulloch stood down as part of the process. In hindsight I did him a favour, since approximately £5m was spent on modernising the mills. Sadly Murray Gordon passed away in 2011 as did Willie Tulloch.

Several challenges were encountered during this buyout but none was as significant as the loss of David Philip who tragically died whilst swimming one morning. In addition to being a great friend, David was my right arm and he had been brought up in a construction background as his father was the main Board director of the Tawse business in Aberdeen before it became Aberdeen Construction Group.

It took a long time to recover and regain focus after his death. George Fraser stepped in and has been a strong support ever since.

We also developed our manpower business Corrie Industrial Services which traded worldwide.

Our manpower portfolio was built up to over 500 men, some engaged onshore at Scottish yards, but also at locations in Singapore, Vietnam, Norway, Southern and Northern Ireland and Western Australia.

Alas this type of business did not marry well with our corporate structures, particularly within McApline, and over the years we ended up downsizing and selling the business.

However we were there first with this spread of expertise and harnessing largely a good quality Scottish and Northern English skill base to represent the United Kingdom throughout the world.

One of the hardest hitting commercial lessons was when we were building a supermarket for Safeways at Crossmyloof in Glasgow. I received a call from one of my Glasgow colleagues on a Friday night, just a few days before the opening to say that the developer, Lesser Land Ltd, had gone bust. I worked over the weekend to quantify what the loss might be. I had been assured by the Glasgow team that it would be in the region of £100-200k. The loss was actually in excess of £1m. I had to have my case for the Bank prepared for the Monday morning. I persuaded the team that we had a plan to recover from the situation, which we effectively did.

I have to pay tribute to the Safeway management team; Stuart Bates and Gordon Weatherspoon from Head Office (near Heathrow) who exercised a 'step in' clause with Lesser Land on the basis that we provided a bank guarantee to underwrite it if something went wrong. We fought the Receivers and delivered the store. Eventually we also collected our money.

Challenges were a common occurrence in those days. We had a housing scheme at Caol in Fort William that had been priced at Head Office in the days of McAlpine. It was another classic mistake and we battled to ensure that the losses were contained. We still ended up losing £600,000 and learned a big lesson about long distance pricing!

It's fair to say that our management buyout (MBO) was quite a startling event for the Highlands. I remember conversing with Fraser Morrison who had gone through the same process with the Shand Group. We compared the parallel paths of two north companies. The Morrison and Tulloch journey in this period of MBO was challenging and fierce. I remember thumping the table and demanding to know why we weren't making the same profit margins as Morrisons.

10. REUNION WITH BANK OF SCOTLAND

Having enjoyed excellent service in years gone by from the Royal Bank of Scotland (in particular from Jim Cooper and Ken Matheson), we decided to tidy up our share structures, and at that point also developed a large joint venture with Bank of Scotland called Tulloch Homes (West) Limited (THWL). We took the assets back under control as a joint venture (JV) and developed them out. This growth effectively made Tulloch appear a lot bigger than it was. The joint venture swamped the main company in terms of turnover.

Our formula was very simple. We sought to buy, reprogramme, plan, build, sell, and pay back the debt. Indeed the JV was a much bigger vehicle than Tulloch itself. It built on a whole range of sites from Cumbria to the central belt of Scotland. This brought us into contact with West based colleagues from Bank of Scotland; Dr Roland Mitchell, Stuart Henderson, and Peter Cummings. They all gave us solid support. We also met an individual who was at the centre of our management on THWL (raising our capital and profile); John Barclay.

When THWL had run its course and sorted out its myriad of sites and developments, it was sold back to Tulloch on the basis that BoS took equity in our vehicle as consideration for their shares in THWL. John Barclay was the representative for BoS. In day to day terms Peter Cummings was more involved and crucial to the sensible decisions required to marshall sites, sometimes for high profile individuals. By 'marshall' I mean that what Peter did avoided any claims from third parties, and recognised the status and position of the individuals themselves.

How did we balance the books? We bought mainstream sites, and we anchored sites in the early days with a 78 unit development at Oban Drive in Glasgow (previously a school purchased from the local authority). Because it was in the West End at the edge of Queen Margaret Drive, it sold very well.

We worked on our housing rescue business in tandem with Kevin McCabe's group which looked after Bank of Scotland interests on the commercial property front. There was always overlap between the groups as Scarborough and Tulloch worked together to resolve the issues on behalf of the bank. There was a common thread woven through all of these relationships to 'pull together'. This attitude is very much missed in today's business world.

Our housing rescue business basically focused on acquiring sites from developers who had hit hard times, and had entered formal insolvency proceedings and required rescue.

In these days the Bank of Scotland were always innovative in terms of how they approached their customers in this perilous state and were very careful to ensure fair play at all times and on many occasions we acquired sites at levels ahead of market values simply to demonstrate that we were being fair, equitable and clean in terms of how these situations were dealt with. Sites we acquired ranged from Glasgow and Ayrshire into North Cumbria as well not far from the Sellafield nuclear plant.

The trick was to build what would sell and pay down debt but to augment we acquired one or two mainstream housing sites bought on the open market to generate sensible margins to create a surplus to cover interest deficits on a distressed portfolio. We achieved this.

John Barclay was excellent and pivotal as a banker also in the Tulloch Homes West scenario, and the eventual merger with Tulloch, but he had a hankering to work on our side of the fence which I firmly rejected.

One of our well known, locally based partners in Inverness could not fulfil their part of what originally was a joint venture obligation to purchase a land mass known as Milton of Leys, but John came up with the goods sitting one Sunday morning after our 25th wedding anniversary celebration in the grounds of Lochardil Hotel. He backed our judgement that the site had the potential to make a lot of money; it did. In some ways John was a tremendous challenge to work with, but we matched him, and always recognised that he played an excellent part in our growth.

However, the unsung hero here was Peter Cummings. He resolutely stayed firm and commercial and is a recognised supporter through our long corporate journey. Stuart Henderson was of a different species. He was 'old school', from Edinburgh, and was probably parachuted into the West of Scotland to check what these guys were up to.

Stuart was chairman of Tulloch Homes (West), and to underpin his involvement we had a board meeting one day in Glasgow at 11am.

I dutifully caught the Logan Air flight from Inverness at 7.15am, but I was late for the meeting because the plane was unable to land. It circled for an hour. I remember the stewardess urging us to adopt the brace position and avoid looking out of the window. Obviously I looked out of the window and saw fire engines racing along the runway. It turned out to be a computer glitch rather than a mechanical failure and we landed safely. However, we were ushered into a debriefing trauma centre where I rapidly made my excuses and left. I was 40 minutes late for the board meeting, but the chairman said the reason was irrelevant and I should 'never be late for board meetings!' It seems that the rules were the rules!

As our relationship with BoS moved to calmer waters we came under the wing of Ian Robertson in Edinburgh, again a great supporter of our cause, and he was never hesitant to rise to a challenge as we grew the business. Sadly Ian died in

2010. This was a great loss to all his clients, but more so to his family.

When the journey for Tulloch Homes (West) was completed, and economy returned to normal, we bought the Bank of Scotland out of their 50% share. We reorganised the share capital, removed Royal Bank of Scotland development capital (and Murray Johnston) and replaced them with the Bank of Scotland. These were interesting days involving interesting characters.

This also brought us into the era of having all our banking controlled in the Central Belt of Scotland. First Glasgow had control before it moved to Uberior House, and then the Mound in Edinburgh. We enjoyed the company and business interaction of some pretty big players such as Roland Mitchell and Ian Robertson. Ian was particularly good to us as a Group in the sense that he trusted our judgement and realised that, although some of our deals were less than conventional, they were still worth progressing.

Even in times of challenge we enjoyed banter and commercial interaction with the banking community; Alan Murray, Andy Betchley, Ray Robertson, Laura Milligan, Douglas Black, Stuart Henderson and many more. Alan became one of our non-execs when he retired from his position as Managing Director of the British Linen Bank. Alan's rule, as a banker, was that when you concluded a deal, the Friday afternoon had to be emptied of commitments so that you could participate in celebratory red wine and pasta at Bar Roma (Edinburgh) with Douglas Black in attendance. It was a good tradition. Alan remained a stalwart and bastion of good common sense before finally retiring from Tulloch in 2010 and most important of all the friendship built up over the years has been maintained.

11. INVERNESS CALEDONIAN THISTLE AND THE PRECIPICE

Without Tulloch, Inverness Caledonian Thistle Football Club (ICT) would have folded!

It had a large debt burden, and no revenue to underpin trading in the first division of the Scottish Football League meant that it was on a rocky road. At the invitation of the Bank of Scotland, we set about rescuing the business from the precipice. Whilst it was a painful process for the brave heroes who had joined the two clubs in the first place, the medicine was urgently needed. I, however, respect Dougie McGillvray and Jock MacDonald for the sterling job they did in bringing the clubs together in the first place. I also fully remember the launch of the club at a lunch where the guarantors of the Plc listing were asked to stand up and these people comprised Ken Thomson, Dougie McGillvray, Roy MacLennan, Willie Main, and Tulloch Group.

Inverness Caledonian Thistle comprised the merger of two local clubs in the Inverness area. Inverness Thistle FC who played their football at Kingsmills Park in Inverness and were run by Jock Macdonald of Tomatin Distillery fame, serviced the population largely to the East of Inverness in and around the Crown, Diriebught, Hilton and Raigmore areas. Inverness Caledonian FC were based at Telford Street wedged between the river area and the canal on the West of the river and adjacent to the then Howdens Garden

Centre and bordered by distilleries such as Glenalbyn, now sadly defunct and redeveloped as a site.

Both clubs had a huge support for their Highland League journeys each year and also had a deep rivalry over the years with periods of domination ebbing and flowing. It was interesting that Clachnacuddin FC, the third force in Inverness, did not come to the party but it was firmly their call not to do so.

Over a protracted period of bickering and discussion the merger fused the two clubs together and to show the level of bickering the Plc was named Inverness Thistle and Caledonian FC Plc and the club traded in the Scottish League system as Inverness Caledonian Thistle FC but both sides were trying to maintain their prominence in the deal.

Sadly the divide issues still exist today with supporters from a certain generational strand, effectively boycotting the Newco which is a shame because the merger propelled the Highlands and Inverness into the Scottish League system and all of a sudden recognition was gained nationwide putting Inverness on the map as a zone.

Over the years many strategies had to be devised to keep focus and stay afloat both financially and in a physical sense.

The simple deal that saw the sale of the stadium, which was then leased back to the football club (now an operating company), was most welcome. The debt was beginning to undermine the club's already tenuous status.

Tulloch injected half a million pounds, and, instead of taking control of the club it limited shareholdings to 29.9%. Under the rules of the Takeover Panel, this was the agreed level it had to stay at. I felt it was important that the community spirit was still in evidence. (A further sum of four million was injected to remove the debt).

During my time as Chairman of Caley Thistle my Deputy, Ken Thomson, was a tower of strength. He was a robust character having lived through the merger of the two clubs, the rescue of the business, the need to inject new capital, and then engineering a sale and a subsequent lease back to the club of the stadium.

At the same time a strategy was written (amidst a few wobbles and headaches) with significant input from my successors, Chairman Ken Mackie, Graeme Bennett, and the manager of team at the time, 'Pele' Paterson. *The Road to Premier League Football*, was finalised and published. Manager John Robertson (ex Hearts striker) finally secured the club the much sought after promotion to the Premier League. Steve Patterson and Duncan Shearer also made significant contributions to the development of Inverness Caledonian Thistle as a force in Scottish Football.

My last stint as Chairman was when we had a challenge to build additional seating when we moved into the Premier League set-up and were playing at Aberdeen Football Club. If we had continued to play our games in Aberdeen the financial challenges would have swamped us again. Although we were very grateful to Stewart Milne and Pittodrie for hosting us, our fan base simply did not justify continuing the process.

With support from The Highland Council we fast-tracked the planning application to build the North and South stands at the Tulloch Caledonian Stadium, and we worked with our building control department to deliver the two new stands within 47 days (which met the deadline), and allowed us to return home to play the rest of our games.

Calling it the Tulloch Caledonian Stadium was a little controversial, but considering we put more than £4m plus into the club why shouldn't Tulloch be proud to display the Tulloch name on our local football stadium? Most of our fans understand this. However that is about to change shortly when the naming rights go out to tender and the Tulloch badge will come off the stadium.

We had some good times and plenty of laughs even at very serious moments; what's the point if you can't laugh at events and at yourself?

To help with the building process the Highland Council Common Good Fund contributed £600,000. However, dialogue with the Chief Exec a few months later brought up the topic of developing Eden Court. We undertook to repay the council, with interest, and yet again Tulloch took on the burden with their investment in Inverness Caledonian Thistle now at more than £5m.

I think my connection with the club led to more spats (football and financial) than any other aspect of my business. We kept on track with Alan Savage taking control of the business with my support, then George Fraser taking over with Alan's support.

I think our sustainability surprised quite a few people in the footballing establishment. We set out to make many changes. In particular we wanted to remove the club from the Plc register to make it a limited company again. We also wanted to balance the books so that income matched expenditure!

We were one of the first clubs to endorse this strategy as a policy and even up to 2014 the club is free from external debt thanks to shareholders and stalwarts. One of the everlasting spots was the naming of the stadium as the Tulloch Caledonian Stadium but after all, Tulloch had injected over £5,000,000+ to the equation and they were entitled to at least ask for the naming rights on the North and South stands which propelled the club into survival mode within the Premier League.

I make no apology for this and as an example of fair play when Jock Macdonald passed away I had no hesitation in agreeing to Jock's name being attached to the main stand as the Jock Macdonald Stand.

To those who abandoned ship over the years we wish them well and it's good to see Inverness Caledonian Thistle prosper in the league and in 2014 end up in the highest place ever gained in 2015.

We mustn't forget Ross County FC either who came into the league system at the same time as us and indeed Tulloch built the Victoria stand for Ross County with my good friend Gordon MacRae as project manager, but as usual the normal cash crisis emerged which meant that Ross County couldn't pay for the last couple of measurements on this so we ended up taking shares in Ross County as an assist to that club also.

When I joined Inverness Caledonian Thistle shares owned by me in Ross County FC had to be sold to a third party to comply with the league rules, but I continuously look to see Inverness Caledonian Thistle FC beat Ross County for it is equally as important that we keep them in the same league as us from a sensible practical revenue viewpoint.

This is particularly so when we have lost the impact on revenue from Rangers FC which in itself probably merits a book, but that is for others.

Now we find ourselves in a situation where public commentary has been made on the state of the English Premiership and Championship. Of course, in Scotland our own Premier League is in a sorry state given the pressure on gate income and the ever increasing demands from the playing fraternity with regard to base salaries. The disappearance of Rangers FC, temporarily, to the 3rd Division was also a blow, and as a result of the debacle my view is that we need a fundamental refresh of our governing body in Scotland.

However, Inverness Caledonian Thistle adopted a different line. It looked for people to play for it, and the shirt. I am pleased to say that the squad we have enjoyed over the years has done so to great effect. ICT is a community club. It is not a ruthless central belt or English outfit. We regard our football as community focussed, and we happen to be playing in the highest league in the land thanks to the hard work of the managers, and the quality and local influence of the playing side.

We're looking to encourage others, via shareholder placing, to take the club forward. I think the time for change is an important factor at whatever level within the club is judged appropriate. We will remain very firm supporters, but we will not feature in the shareholder base. It's time for new blood so that the approaches of the past are not set in stone. The next generation deserves a chance to take it to the highest level in the Scottish League system. At this juncture Muirfield Mills has entered the arena heralding the change signalled above and the future direction of the football club operation.

The highlight of my time with the club was, of course, the 3-1 drubbing of Celtic at Parkhead in the Scottish Cup a number of years ago. It spawned the famous newspaper (*The Sun*) headline 'Super Caley go Ballistic, Celtic are Atrocious.'

On that spectacular night I remember dragging Steve 'Pele' Paterson along the main stand to meet his fans and take the acclaim he so richly deserved.

I flew back from Switzerland for the match. It took me three trains and two flights to get to Glasgow. My suit was sent from Inverness, and we went to the game with a degree of trepidation. We were really just expecting to have a good time, and an evening out on the back of Glasgow Celtic.

The after game party at the Thistle Hotel in Glasgow was immense. I repeated my journey of two flights and three trains when I flew back to Switzerland the next morning sporting a very sore head. I got into the ski resort of Klosters to discover, perversely, that the ski-ing had been called off due to adverse weather conditions. I saw my wife walking down the street. She asked: "What was the score?" I replied: "3-1"

"Not that bad then," she said.

I explained that ICT had trounced Celtic, and we proceed to have a glass or two of champagne to celebrate.

As I tail off the story of Inverness Caledonian Thistle's journey it is also probably relevant to signal that Scottish Football no longer has competition following the demise of Rangers FC, and it is not good for the management of Celtic FC to herald that they don't expect any competition soon. That will turn fans off and will begin to show in the coffers of Celtic FC notwithstanding their excellent runs in Europe. Rangers however are on their way back! Maybe Aberdeen can prove me wrong?

A big magic wand is needed for Scottish Football, and mid-point of 2014 we set sail on the journey with no sponsor for the League, with the television rights a pittance compared to the sums earned in England and, whilst there is good banter and completion between the clubs further down the league we need a complete rethink. The league now has a sponsor, but not at previous levels.

The 2013 rethink was just glossing over the problems and I fully concur with the thought that there was protection for the clubs already in there at a higher level, but the grass roots need to be addressed as well if Scottish Football has any chance of surviving.

Not a pretty sight but I would say the management both at SFA level and at SPFL level need to look in the mirror and have a good think about what they have created and what is not working.

However, perseverance, grit, doggedness, you name it – saw ICT survive in the top flight, move up into the top six ratings and in 2015, peak by ending up 3rd in the league and winning the Scottish Cup.

Now that's real Highland history – a real "Roy of the Rovers" story and a well done to Kenny Cameron, Ken Thompson, the Board, the Team and the support staff. I reflect on these dark days of inappropriate funding and tricks and conclude – didn't they do well!

Across the bridge Roy McGregor deserves plaudits also for the job he has done with Ross County.

Father Adam late 40s in Wick Station

My mother in her Wrens uniform 1943

with mum in 2004

Granny Wick with Catherine and Babs

The family and friends at Dunrobbin Castle

With daughters Tina and Caroline on my 55th Birthday

RT HON CHARLES KENNEDY MP

Personal.

HOUSE OF COMMONS
LONDON SW1A 0AA

December 31st 2005.

Dear David,

Many congratulations upon the award
of the CBE in the New Year Honours.

This is a very fitting recognition of your
huge achievements and contribution over
the years - from business and commerce to
sport and charitable causes. So many
have reason to be grateful to you.

Doubtless our paths will cross at a
local fixture in due course!

With best wishes for 2006 -

Yours ever,

Charles.

David Sutherland, CBE.

Inverness Royal Academy Donna Matheson

BOARD 2006

My maternal Grandfather
William Simpson

Pop with his boys: John, Charles, George, DFS
with Derek seated and Meg the dog

DFS and "the Boss" Anne

Favourite spot Glen Calvie estate with Zag & ARD

London Royal Smithfield Show 2004
Prince Philip of Oldtown
Winner of the Highland Class
Bred by DF & AM Sutherland

Last bullock to win the Royal Smithfield
show with tlc from Bob Tulloch
Shown by Rich Thomson (pictured)
London Royal Smithfield Sow
Prince Philip of Old Town
Winner of the Highland class
Bred by DF & AM Sutherland

Grandfather Donald with Beauty Queen at Wick Gala

12. PROJECT ANCIENT MARINER AND AN ITALIAN AFFAIR

Semple Cochrane Plc, a business portfolio based in Paisley and trading throughout the UK and in Thailand, was a very high profile public company within Scotland and listed on the London stock exchange, i.e. a Plc.

I won't go into people or personalities other than to say that this was a business which was run in a manner different from the norm I'd experienced. They adopted a route of changing banks or, to give it its current terminology, refinanced from Clydesdale to Bank of Scotland. Clydesdale therefore were happy and had all their indebtedness repaid. HBoS were left holding the baby but with help from a few of us the company entered a period of intensive care, reconstruction and a recuperation before it perished.

What happened here was that Kevin McCabe and his team took over the shell of the Plc and the trader was hived down to a new Semple Cochrane.

A lot of noise and bluster occurred around this scenario but at the end of the day the story died.

We were asked by Bank of Scotland to help out at Semple Cochrane. It was backed by the Bank of Scotland on a fast track basis from Clydesdale, but I think it was more likely that effective homework had not been carried out. George Fraser and I hatched a deal in a Chinese restaurant in

Glasgow, The Amber Regent, one evening at a meeting with Kevin McCabe and two executives from Semple Cochrane.

The core of the Semple business was diverse; marine engineering, motorway CCTV, electrics, mechanics, and a whole range of other products that included a business in Thailand focussing on prison security systems.

The Bank of Scotland wanted us to acquire the trader, and for Kevin McCabe to take the Plc, but part of this process involved a reconstruction that dealt with the Semple debt.

We called the project *Ancient Mariner,* and the tombstone on completion of the deal was a fisherman wearing a sou'wester carrying a model of the Titanic under his arm. This miniature model brings a wry smile to my face every time I see it in my study. My wry smile is always relevant as I dreamt up the idea of the *Ancient Mariner* carrying the Titanic under his arm – how apt this proved to be.

The Semple demise was, quite simply, catastrophic, and, being parachuted into this transaction, the Chief Executive at the time was, rightly so, looking after his own exit. The attraction here was that there was a group of very high quality non executives involved, probably at the behest of the Bank of Scotland; they all needed to be removed from the equation as the business moved into private hands. It was a rocky ride and no doubt scores were settled in the years ahead! These non execs didn't realise the extent of the quicksand they sat upon as directors of a hopelessly insolvent corporate vehicle.

The position was far worse than anticipated; the facilities' management arm of the Bank of Scotland promised that we would pick up significant work from them. The work didn't materialise.

In the midst of the Semple rescue, and at a very tricky stage in the evolution of the business, I had a health issue. I had a malignant melanoma, but, ever the planner, I looked ahead and decided that a CEO was top priority for Semple. I was carrying out the role in addition to my main position at Tulloch, but decided I needed more time to look after my own health. I actually did this in four days before returning to Inverness to tell my family about my problem i.e. interview, deal, sign off – bingo – a new chief executive in place – fast track!

I brought in a corporate buccaneer of quality; Gordon McKie (until fairly recently he was chief exec of Scottish Rugby and is now Chief Exec of the Hong Kong Football Association). He was a turnaround specialist and he was to drive our strategy forward. However, the more I protested to Ray Robertson at Bank of Scotland about the lack of HBOS workload, the more my objections fell on deaf ears. Ian Robertson instructed me to sell my shares to the management; I readily agreed. George and I picked up £250,000 for our efforts, and Gordon managed to hold the business together for a year before it ceased to exist. Who knows, perhaps that was the game plan, but we retreated with dignity.

Around the same time we were approached by Gladedale PLC which was run by a corporate operator called Remo Dupre. Remo offered us £36m for our housing business. We agreed to this on the grounds that he did not "chip" the transaction price. What did he do? He chipped it on something that was totally incorrect. However, being pragmatic in my own mind we told Remo to take a hike, and withdrew the business from sale. He had gone through full diligence and had even announced to the market that he was buying it. I went to see my 41% shareholder, the Bank of Scotland, and told them I was pulling the deal because Remo had chipped it. They replied that he needed us and our management, and they wanted us (as co shareholders), to complete the deal. I refused.

A terse and heated conversation took place between us and Ray Robertson. Ian Robertson then summoned me saying: "I've got some very unhappy campers in my team because you are not toeing the party line on this transaction. We don't think we should remain shareholders." I remember the hair on the back of my neck standing on end before he hesitated and said: "I want you to buy us out of Tulloch, what do you think it's worth?"

I provided a low figure and couldn't believe that he was being so helpful. I was silent. He said: "I suppose you would like me to fund this buyout?" Hey presto, we hammered out a deal that enabled us to buy out the Bank of Scotland, and once again have 100% ownership.

All of this was carried out in a spirit and intent basis, and at all times the bank remained loyal and pragmatic in their handling of our account. The respect was mutual.

My first encounter with Remo was when he owned a company called Fairbriar. It spectacularly crashed in the late 1990s. It was one of the first administrations in the UK to be handled by Ernst and Young.

Kevin McCabe was sent in by Bank of Scotland to advise, and occasionally Kevin would invite me to one of the Administrators' meetings. He reluctantly conceded that I knew more about house building than he did (at that point)!

The Gladedale dialogue brought us into the South East market; as Remo showed me around his empire I realised that I could do that too. I set out to find a partner and Stephen Brazier appeared. Coincidentally he was recommended by Kevin McCabe. The two of us set up Argyll Developments. We traded in and around the M25, building houses from Edenbridge in Kent, right round to Watford and dazzling places such as Gerrards Cross, Beaconsfield and Crawley near Gatwick.

I believe that revenge is a dish best served cold and I confess that I did enjoy buying a site in Epsom close to Remo's head office and placing a massive Argyll Developments sign on it. I see it as poetic justice but I still haven't had the chance to debate it with him and to thank him for the idea.

This period of change led me to understand that the most important business relationship will always be the one that you have with your bank. Over the years we have been very fortunate to forge and maintain good working relations with them. We were guided and supported through the Famco Tulloch situation in Saudi Arabia, the indigestion inflicted by Semple, and our rejection of Remo Dupre's approach to buying the housing business. Thank you to both Bank of Scotland and Royal Bank of Scotland

13. THE SALE OF THE THREE 3'S TO ROK PLC IN 2006

In late spring 2006 I received a cold call at the Glasgow office from an individual, Colin McEachern, who was acting for Rok Plc. He wanted an urgent meeting. George and I did our homework on Rok and discovered that they were a growing business based in the South West of England. They were headed by a very energetic Chief Executive, Garvis Snook. Even in these early days the company was signalling 'world domination' in terms of the local builder role in the UK. The strapline was 'the nation's local builder'.

We met with Colin who said that Garvis Snook had sent him to ascertain if we were willing to sell our business, which by this time included mainstream construction, civil engineering, plant hire, house building, and various other components. We met with Garvis Snook who wanted to buy the construction, civils, and services elements. The construction business had quite a high turnover, was profitable and cash generative. The civil engineering was also profitable and generated a lot of cash, and our burgeoning services business was expanding throughout Scotland and trading under the Corrie banner. Construction, civils, and Corries were the origin of the three C's badge.

We negotiated hard and drove out a price of £31.3m. Part of the package also included us passing our final pension salary scheme to Rok; it was in deficit. However, the deal did not run smoothly and there was a wobble that caused me to take a step back and refuse to proceed. Again this was an attempt by Rok Plc to chip down the price.

Throughout my life I've had the occasional petulant moment where I have dug in my heels. What I didn't know at the time was that Garvis Snook was holed up with his Board in Newcastle where they spent five hours debating whether I would call to say I'd changed my mind. I stood my ground. When Garvis finally called me I was at the Holyrood Hotel in Edinburgh having just returned from a meeting hosted by Donald Macdonald with Alex Salmond and Jack McConnell (separately) on a charitable issue in Malawi. As an aside we called the meetings 'chalk and cheese' because Alex Salmond was streets ahead of Jack McConnell in terms of his vision and enthusiasm for what we were trying to do in Malawi. Meantime, down in Newcastle, Rok conceded to my way of thinking! The completion meeting was held in October at the offices of McLay Murray and Spens in London a week later, but at the last minute there was another hitch.

A pension issue arose late in the evening and I decided to phone Sandy Grant, my Finance Director, to confirm some facts. I rang Sandy's mobile and house; he didn't answer despite an instruction to all concerned to keep their lines open.

What do I do? I'm in London, it's late at night, and I needed clarification. I phoned Kenny Cameron (I knew he was a late bedder) and asked him to go to Sandy's house at Milton of Leys. With a degree of trepidation Kenny motored up to Sandy's (a Tulloch bungalow aptly named the Sutherland), rang the bell, and was greeted at the door by Maree Grant, Sandy's wife. Kenny was invited in to find Sandy sitting up in bed. Kenny gingerly asked him to phone me which he dutifully did!

Sandy and I discussed the business at hand but the pensions issue was still on the table. We had to get the pension trustees out of bed at 1am to ratify the position. I crawled back to Gatwick airport on the staff train at 4am, and had to get up early to catch the first flight to Inverness with the deal in the bag. They paid us £31.3m, £9m of that in shares, and by this mechanism we became the largest shareholders in Rok, and I joined the Board. I have to say that my time there was very uncomfortable, not least because I started to highlight areas of concern that I had experience of from my own career. I'm sure the Chairman repeatedly thought 'how dare this upstart challenge my Chief Executive?!'

By autumn 2007 I realised that I was battering my head against a brick wall; regardless of what I said the other non execs clearly saw me as little more than a pain. I resigned.

The ethical question was brought to the fore here in that we clearly had a Board where the non-execs were not listened to and frankly one would naturally look at the leadership, stewardship, etc and ask why the Chairman wasn't more challenging. This was publicly blown out by the plight of Rok Plc when it hit the buffers much sooner than others in the period of financial crisis running from 2008, but also says that the blind faith put in certain members of the team by the Chief Exec was misguided and contributory.

They went bust in 2010. I dug out the correspondence I'd had with the Chairman (and others); these reports were relevant and damning. Chief Executive, Garvis Snook, was the man who drove all the acquisitions. On one acquisition he challenged me, claiming that I didn't know the difference between an exec and a non exec. I was right. He was wrong on the issue I raised.

It was sad to see all of our old colleagues thrown on the job scrapheap so close to Christmas. Thankfully most of them secured new work quickly.

When we concluded our original deal and ingathered £23m+ in cash we did not distribute it to our shareholders. We retained it to help boost our land bank within the housing division. Hindsight suggests that perhaps that wasn't the best decision, but once it had been made we stuck to it.

Post acquisition we still traded with Rok and they carried out a great deal of our construction work in the North of Scotland. By this time George Fraser was Rok's Managing

Director. He was supported by Donald Mackenzie, Sandy Grant and Kenny Cameron.

In 2007, and settling down from the Rok transaction in 2006, the Homes business started to generate significant profit (largely land sales and the base homes trading portfolio). Each year we sold one or two sites that generated the bulk of the profits (ie not the volume build).

Our expansion involved amongst others the acquisition of Cameron and Patterson, a small Dingwall based housebuilder and we enjoyed the support of Alan Cameron and Kenny Patterson.

14. MIDDLE EASTERN APPROACH

Following the sales of the 3C's (construction, civils, and Corries) to Rok in 2006 we set about building up the homes business with great assistance from the Bank of Scotland. BoS recognised our desire to be able to float the business, or secure an Aim listing. In March 2007, six months post the Rok deal, I received a surprise phone call from a previous shareholder representative, Joe McGrane. I had first met him when he was Managing Director of Royal Bank Development Capital Limited. Joe had called to ask me if he could purchase a controlling stake in our business.

We carried out diligence via Deloitte. Simultaneously we produced a corporate DVD. The opening shot was an aerial view of Dunrobin Castle outside Brora with some good ethereal Scottish music as the soundtrack. Joe indicated that when the DVD was shown in the Bahrain Boardroom his Arab colleagues were mega enthusiastic about this type of investment in Scotland. They couldn't believe they were fortunate enough to have such an opportunity.

They made a substantial offer for 60% of the business, and, with help from Joe's assistant George McRitchie (who sadly died in 2011), we moved swiftly to legals. We were within a whisker of settling the deal at the end of summer when the gulf went quiet. There was no communication for three weeks. The silence was deafening. We kept Bank of Scotland informed on progress. However, the last point, which I think might have had a bearing on this, was the intellectual challenge presented to us by Sharia Finance. This had deep, and admirable, principles that had potentially significant implications for Tulloch as a housebuilder in the Highlands of Scotland.

The Bank of Scotland was shadowing our every move. One day they agreed to step into the breach. In late October 2007, and flowing from the 'no deal' process, HBOS, who had expressed an interest in assisting us with our strategic objectives, asked for a diligence refresh exercise. It was fast tracked by Deloitte, and an offer emerged by Christmas. We negotiated a compromise on the pricing and a completion meeting was held in April 2008. We were asked to hold back on releasing this information to the media so that another deal could be concluded. In hindsight we judged that the other deal was Miller, the Edinburgh based construction house building and property company. 2008 became a year of real challenge!!

What had happened was in the Autumn of 2008 signals were around which suggested a financial crash, whereby banks and institutions purchased bundles of assets where at the core some of the assets were not underpinned by covenants of the correct strength, and these assets were worth billions of pounds but were toxic and needed significant write down to reflect the true value on the balance sheets of the banks who purchased them.

The practice kept going for a long time and certain banks were actually buying back bundles of subprime from institutions they had sold into previously. By the Autumn of 2008 it became a real car crash much bigger and more toxic than the great depression of the 1930s and it continued to build up momentum putting a lot of the Western economies in jeopardy.

The HBOS logic in taking a stake in a house builder such as Tulloch was:

a) To assist us to exit or float within two to three years' time. We had a good track record of delivering corporate transactions and exit.

b) They owned Britain's largest mortgage bank (the Halifax), and it seemed like a good idea to link. The Halifax mortgage products were pivotal for our sales teams (and many other house builders).

c) None of us could foresee the events of late autumn 2008. How often do we wish for foresight and preach hindsight!

The deal concluded that Uberior Ventures should take a 40% stake in our business, again. The nature of the stake has changed complexion since 2008 somewhat!

This means that, under pressure from markets in the surveying profession, property carry values were depressed. The door was opened for many banks to take the opportunity, as part of a refinancing examination, to instigate mechanisms which enhanced their control of balance sheets.

The end game and progression for Tulloch business in this was an ignominious bundling into a project called Project Lundy. A hair cut was offered on debt. The idea was for many companies to get together to move away large sums of indebtedness approaching £1 billion.

Many companies were parcelled together and offered to hedge funds, based largely overseas, to acquire and marshall out the residual businesses with a much reduced debt burden.

The irony of this from a house building viewpoint is that if the momentum had been maintained, and faith maintained that recovery would eventually occur, loads of banks might have got larger chunks of their money back. But alas that was not to be the case as banks rushed to repair their balance sheets, take the pain of government assistance and try to return to normality.

15. THE BUBBLE BURSTS AND THE ROAD TO RECOVERY

As we moved through 2008 we began to notice some 'creaking' in the mortgage availability for our customers. Cancellation rates increased. The snowball began to gain momentum in late October when it became obvious that our banking system was under severe strain; this was largely caused by sub-prime mortgages (initially in the States), running through to a full blown credit crunch where banks weren't lending to each other and LIBOR (London InterBank Offered Rate) pricing rocketed. The final picture became clearer; we were staring at the deepest recession we had experienced in our business lifetime. It was deeper than that of the late 1920s, which of course we are all too young to remember!

All hell broke loose in October. HBOS (now taken over by LBG) and Royal Bank of Scotland both needed help from the Government. Whilst this chaos was going on Tulloch and their customers were frozen in a time warp. We were doing our best in challenging circumstances, but mortgages were almost unobtainable and our house sales were plummeting. We continued to build however and somehow found finance for clients to buy our products.

I think we handled the crisis well. We increased our low cost output from circa 50 units to 150 units. We flattened our sales presences in the Glasgow area, but kept on the Aberdeen and Inverness build out and sell out. In 2009 we refinanced our business with help from Lloyds Banking Group (LBG), who by this time had absorbed HBOS. The refinancing involved a debt equity swap which helped to rebuild our Balance Sheet so that we could tackle the future with some confidence.

Our land bank did not suffer the rigours of many land banks in the south and midlands of England and Scotland. Most of it was in the Inverness zone, and we had some excellent strategic purchases over the years that would stand the business in good stead for the future by generating excellent gross margins.

On that note, I read with interest an article from a senior director at Lloyds Banking Group who I once had the pleasure of meeting. He stated that bankers should be there in good and bad times to help you plan your balance sheets and prepare for the future (without always looking to the past). I think Tulloch has a lot of history, and to use the words of my good friend Robert Smith (at a pre Camanachd Cup Final in 2010), 'we've come a long way', even in banking terms.

Since 2008 we have had a real challenge to work with. Our working relationship with the bank changed fundamentally, and we had a regimented recovery programme to follow. Most of 2009 was fine as we embarked on a journey to refinance our facilities with LBG. This journey included an independent business review (IBR). The review disregarded our long relationship with HBOS. Lloyds Banking Group saw every risk as 'new'.

The independent business review was an expensive process. It was carried out by KPMG in Edinburgh. To back it up, we also had a firm of commercial valuers who were asked to look at the valuation position from a domestic house building point of view.

This review was a tortuous process to say the least. The professionals were doing their job, but the process cost us nearly £3m (not including internal staff time). The cost came at a time when we could least afford it, and the quantity of time senior management had to spend on it was horrendous (and questionable in terms of our end goal).

The outcome emerged; a debt equity swap. It was very considerate of the bank, and gave us the Balance Sheet strength via the introduction of a preference share to maintain momentum. The policy therefore was to hold for recovery.

However, our customers still couldn't secure mortgages and lacked the confidence and means to buy. Somehow, in the Highlands, we continued to build and sell, albeit at a more modest level. In years gone by we would have naturally sold land, but we were unable to because nobody had the resources to buy.

The local authority in Inverness, The Highland Council and its CEO, Alistair Dodds, demonstrated a firm grasp of the situation by hosting a conference to discuss the credit crunch. During this process came a full understanding that the council, and its partners in the housing associations, would accelerate funding commitments for affordable housing. This arrangement kept the sub contractors and tradesmen busy for the bulk of 2009.

Tulloch Homes Group Limited, through our Tulloch Homes Express vehicle, increased our affordable activity from 50 to 150 within the space of six months. We continued to bring forward our section 75 sites, with funding from the Scottish Government. However, in terms of the house building sector, we were not out of the dip. We were running on a ratio of circa 50%. We were selling below 200 private units a year; we should have been 350 on our original business plan. My belief is that the Tulloch land is curing all the time, and when the brakes come off, the pent up demand for a place to live will be very obvious in the Highlands. Tullochs will be in a good position to satisfy that need.

In general, I think we did have a good business, we had good people within the business, and we had locations on which to build our product that people wanted to buy. Tulloch has unstintingly contributed to this process via our shared equity scheme which helped people on the property ladder. We introduced a package (properties at Milton of

Leys, Inverness, for £99k with some assistance) for first time buyers, a sector that was wholly ignored in 2008 and 2009.

In terms of political correctness we need the austerity to be out of the way. I don't think any of us doubt that we need to correct the spending imbalance inherited from the past. None of us can apportion blame for the actions of the previous government when it attempted to rescue the financial system; it did what it had to do to avoid Armageddon! However funding for low cost housing has largely dried up and as an industry we needed to think quickly on our feet to maintain momentum. Our City Homes product certainly did that.

I will however never forgive some of the pessimists around the Tulloch issue and it's a pity that HBoS weren't nationalised along with Royal Bank of Scotland prior to the merger with Lloyds which some say was forced. Lloyds TSB were hailed as a bank with little subprime exposure, the real 'steady Eddies' at the helm on the High Street, and leading their banking efforts. Why did they buy HBoS?

What drove this? Ego methinks! Or some form of political intervention or both? One day the story will be told.

16. SUBPRIME, CREDIT CRUNCH AND QUANTITATIVE EASING – A WHOLE NEW VOCABULARY

In 2007 there were several indications that all was not well in the market. In particular the queues outside Northern Rock sounded alarm bells across financial services the world over.

Bear Sterns in the States also had to be dealt with by the US central Bank known as the Fed, and in 2008, late into the cycle, Lehman's (also in the States), dived into bankruptcy.

On our home shores we witnessed the Royal Bank of Scotland, and HBoS carry out rights issues in response to exposure fears from sub-prime, and the reluctance of other banks to lend to each other. Whilst these rights issues were carried out in the summer of 2008 they did not stem the tide which resulted that autumn in LBG taking control of HBoS, and the Royal Bank becoming state owned. Why did they go ahead with the ABN Ambro deal?

Wow! Did we need to understand the meaning of sub-prime and the crisis? Bundles of mortgages were packaged, sliced, diced and sold to unsuspecting traders. All of which were given triple-A ratings by the financial ratings agencies. These went sour, and the consequences are clear for all to see. These financial agencies are now all getting their revenge by downgrading banks and countries.

We watched in amazement as the Government and the Bank of England produced all of the usual economic tricks, such as quantitative easing, following through to austerity.

The British house building market halved in volume overnight, and the United States suffered even more. In the Highlands we could, at least, realise that there was demand for our product. Instead of choosing to stop building in late 2008 (as was suggested by one of our Board co-shareholder representatives) we carried on throughout the crisis, and, more importantly, continued to sell robustly, given the circumstances.

As indicated the Tulloch business became part of a phenomenon known as the 'housing bubble' where the house price curve kept on rising, people somehow managed to borrow more and more money, sometimes on mortgages of 150% of value. Then prick!! – the bubble burst.

That's the theory, but I'd say in the Highlands of Scotland, whilst supply suffered some deflation in house pricing terms, it didn't add up to a bubble burst as it was well known and trailed, and in Inverness for example, the capital of the Highlands, we still traded at respectable levels and our gross margins held up.

The challenge was how to get mortgages for our customers but we addressed that also.

All through the period of house price uncertainty builders made money, as did land owners, and purchasers were all in good jobs paying tax to the exchequer. In addition there was a feeding frenzy of economic activity and growth portrayed by successive governments, both Conservative and Labour.

I can't help feeling that somebody should have rung the alarm bell well before 2008 from a political perspective but nobody heard any bells, at least not in our industry.

However, the old adage of 'cash being king' came to the fore and we managed our business for cash. As time progressed we were in a position where we didn't need to buy more land. Our day-to-day business was very cash positive; all its gross margins were maintained at very acceptable levels across the trading platforms.

We had an investment business that held strategic land, joint ventures and investments. Following the onslaught in 2008-2009 we have turned the majority of these joint venture opportunities, and indeed one major land tranche, into excellent prospects with real value that complemented the business base (still throwing off cash). This meant that we kept our lines clear, and settled down to a run of around 200 houses per annum. Most of these houses are in the Highlands.

The crisis that unfolded in autumn 2008 was the most frightening I have seen in my lengthy career. I'm proud to be able to remind my team that (with the help of Lloyds Banking Group) we survived and I am also pleased to say that, post my departure, Tulloch have continued on track.

Departure for me meant a simple realisation that times had changed. We were now ruled by the bank. I was not prepared to work with people who weren't open and above board in terms of their strategy.

I engineered my departure by indicating that I felt the business didn't need my skills full time as the management team were perfectly well qualified to transact. It would be a saving for the business, though I might say I had voluntarily reduced my salary significantly in 2008.

Flowing on from there I was asked to stay on as a non-executive director which I did but to give George and his team breathing space I decided not to attend meetings but more act in an advisory role to George as he moved through the process of absorbing control.

That soon came to an end and my shares were put in play at a very low level and, apart from two brief months back on the board, my long association with the business terminated.

17. CHARITABLE PAYBACK OVER THE YEARS

I firmly believe in Corporate and Social Responsibility (CSR), and always considered the principle of giving something back to the community was a priority. Tulloch has supported a vast number of good causes that are way too numerous to mention in full.

It was most pleasing to receive a CBE from Her Majesty the Queen in 2006 for services to charity.

We were approached by Dr Finlay Kerr, the 'pipe playing' (former) senior cardiac consultant at Raigmore Hospital in Inverness. He asked us for help to raise money to build a new gym and treatment centre for heart patients. We approached this with great enthusiasm and organised a charity dinner and ball for the British Heart Foundation which raised £90,000. We even auctioned a house; in those days auctioning a house was a feasible plan!

From 1979 onwards Candy Dundas (a Glasgow based charity co-ordinator) persuaded me to support up to four Variety Club coaches. They were given to communities to help transport people to functions and local projects they would otherwise be unable to attend. We supplied coaches from Easterhouse to Alness. The Alness academy pupils came to see us on a school trip one day when we had Jackie Bird from BBC Scotland doing some private TV work for us. It was fabulous to see the reaction of the children, and really helped us to appreciate how important the coach was to them. We also sponsored a coach in Caithness in partnership with Moray Firth Radio's Cash for Kids Project where I was a Trustee.

We were regularly met with pleas for help from schools, football teams, pensioner groups and youth groups. Tulloch met the need wherever possible.

One of the most significant donations we made was to Blythswood care project in deepest Romania. We enjoyed a strong relationship with Blythswood. It's an amazing organisation that is willing to tackle (effectively and with care) the issues that no-one else will touch.

One of the most heart rending challenges we became involved with was a custody battle which a local journalist brought to my attention via her connection as a friend of the family.

A young girl had been removed from her mother's custody and care in Scotland and was taken overseas by her father to Indonesia.

A BBC programme highlighted the plight of the family.

We listened to the story and decided that Tulloch could make a donation and also introduce an individual who had experience of such situations. He in turn enlisted support from a colleague in Australia and the Australian leg of the mission was tasked with carrying out a reconnaissance mission to identify the exact whereabouts of the missing girl.

On the second night of our Australian friend's mission, on an island called Sulawasei he went for a stroll from his hotel; he was ambushed by a belligerent crowd. The date was September 2001 and the crowd were hostile to Americans! Once the Aussie convinced them of his nationality they backed off and with help from a Hindi pilot he flew to Bali and then home.

However he found the girl and her father living in a house boat in a remote village and a plan was hatched and brokered to, effectively, transfer the girl to Kuala Lumpur.

The British end of the family team accompanied by Mum flew to KL for a tearful reunion and contact was made with the British Embassy who helped facilitate the return to the UK.

The Highland reaction to this event was met with encouragement and amazement that this long running story had been brought to a safe and happy conclusion.

On a personal basis it was heartening to see this unfold, a true example of real corporate social responsibility in terms of Tulloch Construction's involvement, and I pay tribute to the family, their two special friends for their successful efforts, and currently the little girl is now a young woman living happily in Scotland close to her family.

I was proud of the ability of our company to help rescue this little girl from the jungles of Sulawesi. It's this type of ordeal that tugs at my heart; there was no way I could refuse the request. It is fortunate that we had two ex Special Forces contacts that we could call on. I pay tribute to them for their successful efforts. The young lady's family are aware of this publication and supported the process of enlightenment.

On a more sedate basis, we help raise funds for village halls, sponsored runs, and even during the credit crunch of 2009, whilst we weren't really in a fit state to continue the good work of Tulloch, I made sure that we honoured any previous commitments; sometimes this meant tapping into my private resources. We were active in donating throughout the UK, Malawi, Romania, and Kerala in South India, and we proudly supported the Highlands Disabled Sport Association in an attendance at an event in Birmingham, flying down and back on a chartered Flybe jet.

Since the millennium we've chosen, privately as a family, to make a significant charitable contribution to Hilton Church Manse which has since been converted into a day centre for pensioners. It doubles up as a youth centre in the evenings. We placed a plaque inside the door in memory of my mother who had enjoyed social support from Hilton Church. She died in 2004.

In 2012, raising funds for the Archie Foundation, at the invitation of the Inverness Courier, was top of my agenda. The proceeds from this book are part of these efforts. The Archie Foundation's mission is to refurbish and modernise the children's ward at Raigmore Hospital so that the standard matches the excellent medical, surgical and nursing care. The charity itself is based in Aberdeen but the funds are being kept in the Highlands. It promotes itself with the strap-line 'making a difference'. I am convinced that it will make a difference. I must be mad because I also completed the New York Marathon in October 2011 on behalf of Archie, and in the relentless pursuit of fundraising. Although the financial climate is a challenge, we are committed to this until 2014. We've worked alongside hospitals before and once had a five year relationship with Breast Cancer Care in Glasgow to help raise funds and awareness. We've also worked closely with the Highland Hospice in Inverness by contributing to their Mount Everest style fund-raising efforts. Local charities touch the hearts of many families, and we love to support them wherever possible.

In 2015, being inextricably linked to the Archie cause, which set sail in Inverness in 2013/14, I was persuaded out of retirement to help Archie's £2million Highland Children's Unit Appeal reach the finishing line. By then, building on the initial fund-raising success, a new budget and target and new thinking had been introduced by NHS Highland so that rather than upgrading the ward at Raigmore, their plan was to create a brand new ward.

I've survived many a knock on this one, ie the Archie Journey, and when you are striving to achieve different outcomes, that is when you see who the true grit characters are – the patients and their families as well as their doctors and nurses.

However, we are approaching the finishing line at long last and to achieve the final lap, we have taken on an exciting group of business-focused individuals who are striving to drive this project over the line. It is so pleasing to see the sheer delight on the faces of people who use the existing facilities, whether they be children or parents, who commend the medical and nursing and ancillary care to all who would like to listen.

I look forward to the new facility being built by the greatest rivals Tulloch ever had – Morrisons – come to fruition.

Across the fence our "Food for Families Project" is now in its fourth year producing over 2,500 meals per year for needy families.

From a humble start, using mince from our beef herd with an army of church-orientated volunteers to produce the food, we now spread the project benefits throughout the Highlands to Easter Ross, Nairn, etc. as well as Inverness.

The 2014/15 winter was also a very interesting experiment in that we expanded the menu and also the organisations who help us and, whilst it was extremely pleasing to have the input from the Muslim community in terms of the vegetarian offerings, it was also humbling to see that Inverness prison and their guests were so enthusiastic, adding to the range of dishes such as macaroni, leek and potato soup, pasta, etc. reflecting the needs of some of our recipients.

The Food for Families has been a truly rewarding experiment and I am ever grateful to Paul and Alex at the Highland Homeless Trust for all the help they have given. Tesco too – 400 turkey dinners last year were donated by Tesco Nesside.

On the business front we've been active with the charities of Prince Charles. In particular we sponsored a number of events for the Prince's Scottish Business Youth Trust. The Prince of Wales formed a company, North Highland Initiative, which effectively continued his grandmother's love for the area. She had a great interest in the north of Scotland, and loved to retreat to her holiday home, the Castle of Mey, near Thurso.

North Highland embarked on a number of ambitious projects given the scale of community life in the Highlands. Some of the meetings around these were very humorous. I was summoned to a grand dining room at Birkhall to discuss one of the Prince's latest strategies. Prince Charles was chairing the meeting and the room was populated by approximately 20 other people. Carol Buxton of Highlands and Islands Enterprise made two fatal mistakes that morning. First she arrived late. She apologised profusely and took her seat. The Prince's irked manner subsided slightly. Unfortunately for Carol, a few moments later her mobile phone rang. If looks could annihilate then Carol would have been annihilated. She apologised once more.

Being a humorous sort I passed a note to her stating that her beheading would occur at noon. She did everything she could to prevent herself from bursting out laughing, thankfully, she succeeded!

18. PEOPLE PEOPLE PEOPLE

Tulloch has come such a long way! The company was in the jaws of death in the Saudi Arabian Joint Venture, and then fell into some very tricky corporate situations where challenging contracts went wrong. It acquired companies, disposed of companies and kept afloat.

One of our best acquisitions and disposals was with Everwarm (and our good friends Bob and Kenny). We purchased the company, grew it over a two year period and resold to a customer at a significant uplift with Michael McMahon transferring as part of the deal.

Michael McMahon, Lydia Graham, and Kenny Saunders have interestingly restarted the Everwarm brand in the central belt of Scotland. I wish them luck. More recently they reversed into a London based plc called Lakeheath.

Considering Tulloch's humble beginnings in the town of Nairn, it built itself up to a turnover of just under £350m. At one point it was generating profits of £10m per annum. This was all down to the hard work of the employees and the people around the business, particularly from the 1980s onwards.

I've had the pleasure of working with a whole range of people from all walks of life. The Tulloch family was a challenge which I think we, in the first instance, found quite daunting. Sometimes disarray gives you the confidence to know that you can make a tangible difference. It was hard to persuade the family to eradicate old, traditional work practices that no longer served the business, but we got there.

David Philip, however, was an excellent supporter and a well respected individual. He became the face of Tulloch construction throughout the Highlands and Islands and after the purchase in 1989 of our management buyout. It was a great personal and business loss when he died at just forty seven after suffering a heart attack.

George Fraser put his shoulder to the wheel when David Philip died. He spawned out of David's era and quickly moved through the ranks to become one of Scotland's foremost contractors and businessmen.

Kenny Cameron, Neil Cameron, Donald MacKenzie, Donnie Fraser, Charlie Monks and Billy Mackay became the backbone of the business in real growth years. They supported us on that journey. Most of us have stayed in regular contact ever since.

I've been privileged to work with some amazing people. Every business needs a team and every business needs individuals who adapt to the business practices in place and deliver the returns required to reinvest. We've had a few 'bad eggs', but we were always fast to re-train or eliminate.

The real stars of Tulloch, in my opinion, are the girls who kept me in order. I needed a lot of attention as I was always darting all over the place. My diary had to be kept in check and these 'guardians of the serpents nest' were excellent: Marjory Robinson, Anne Bruce, Marjory Trace, Meryl Johns, Alyson Marshall, Laura Murray, Rachel Murray and Liz Lowrie. A few others helped at various stages on the journey, notably Abigail (Field Marshall Montgomery), Joyce McNab and Lorna Cameron.

I am eternally grateful to all of the team players who supported me, and to everyone who I worked with on joint ventures. In my period of stewardship I could not have moved ahead without good people behind me such as Kevin McCabe, Donald Macdonald, Muir Mackay, the late Mike Mackenzie, Scott Strachan, Ferdinand Hinteregger, David Cameron, and many more. There are too many names to mention; they know who they are.

The contribution of these people is indelibly tattooed on my brain, and I fully recognise that I was just one cog in the business wheel. Before I retired the next generation of managers was beginning to emerge at Tulloch. I wish them all good luck.

It has been very pleasing to have forged strong connections with such professional, skilled advisers throughout the UK.

For me the journey started with John C Frame & Co in Inverness. It was also significant that, in the early days, the advice of Harry Brown and Andrew Duncan was pivotal in our forward planning. They advised us on the sale of the first family shareholding to Royal Bank Development Capital, and the sale on buy back from Alfred McAlpine Plc.

Also, Ian Bankier has been around Tulloch for about 20 years. He's risen from being a young, thrusting corporate lawyer in Glasgow to a non-exec position and a successful full-blooded businessman in his own right with an 18 strong Whisky Shop chain. His counsel is always most welcome and I declare that I was, until recently, a shareholder in the Whisky Shop chain trading throughout the UK.

Most recently the corporate mantel has been taken on by Donnie Munro of Harper MacLeod in Glasgow. He's had pivotal input into progress over the years, filling Ian Bankier's shoes and then some. Caroline Sutherland and Gary Campbell also grasped the vast real estate portfolio under the control of Tulloch in legal terms and now the enlarging private empire.

When we were part of Alfred McAlpine we met Les Platts and Philip Johnstone who headed up the Manchester operations for Deloitte. At that time, and following the disposal of the business from McAlpine to Tulloch, we recognised that, by this time, Frame Kennedy and Forrest (the company who emerged from John C Frame & Co) were too small to execute a business such as ours. We gravitated back to Deloitte.

We moved from Les Platts in Manchester to Ralph Adams in Edinburgh, and eventually James Baird and David Crawford. David was actually based in Belfast for Deloitte. Over the years they have all been pretty active in terms of marshalling obligations on audit, and tax compliance.

On the corporate finance front Ian Steele, previously Deloitte's global corporate finance partner, is now back in Scotland as senior partner. His input on the corporate front was very important. The advice and professional support that we've had with regard to diligence, acquisitions and disposals, are all held in the greatest esteem. In terms of architectural design, all the professionals have worked on a sterling basis for Tulloch, but Ian Ferguson of ADF (Glasgow based architects), and Allan Rennie of Bracewell Stirling, really stand out as individuals who gave us service way above and beyond the call of duty.

As a matter of public record I'd now like to thank all the professional advisers who have helped to take Tulloch to the position that it is in today, and akin to our JV linkages, they know who they are.

I start with the Tulloch Family themselves who were really a disparate bunch of brothers who had the bones of an excellent business and I hope, with my help, and indeed the help of the other members of the team, the family achieved their ambitions for their efforts over the years.

The philosophy of Alexander Tulloch Senior was clearly for the young to receive a basic education and then go on to full time work, and the five brothers started their journey in life in that mode. As soon as the brothers reached 15 it was into the business, and sometimes a trade was contrived just to sustain a job for a family member.

The management teams from the old days, too huge to mention, had stars, some who moved away and some who stayed the course.

My maxim as an individual has always been that without people you don't have a business and from time to time you also need to 'check and balance' guys and girls, non execs in particular, who double check your strategic drive.

Ian Bankier was the largest player in this field and whilst he started life as our corporate lawyer he never failed to challenge our strategy which was good, positive and demanded a coherent response to his questions.

Alan Murray was not far behind that in the sense that he approached it from a banking perspective with an even more robust direct approach than Ian!

I have continuing tremendous respect for both individuals, and they have played their part in the real growth curve of

Tulloch over the years, particularly the period from the 80s onwards.

Again it is an old adage that in business you meet friends and probably one of the closest I have had is Kevin McCabe who was a long term customer, and I always remember when David Philip died suddenly it was Kevin that came to the fore, took an investment and came on the board to help me steer through these torrid times.

We had our first career non exec in the form of James Haan who made his pile in a range of business units, but was most famous for being involved in the FJC Lilley debacle in Glasgow prior to receivership and moved on to become chairman of British Nuclear Plc, steering it through a very difficult political and environmental gap. James was introduced by Norman Murray, an individual who went onto chair some of the largest Plc's in Scotland as did his boss when the first institutional investment came into Tulloch, Lord Smith of Kelvin.

I am sure that James would have said that Tulloch was not as daunting as British Nuclear, but my memories of James are that he was a tremendous thinker and somebody who looked at the practicalities of the situation. I always remember a job for Hanover Housing Association in Fort William which was priced by McAlpines in Chester and inherited by us as part of our management buyout. To cut a long story short the job lost at the end of the day £600,000 which was a lot of money in 1989 but the problem, as well as production control, was the weather and James had this brainwave when, on one occasion, we took the board to see the site, and they asked why we had not put a tent around the houses we were building. A lot of my colleagues laughed at that but when you think back that is the way, provided the job could stand the cost of it, that you eliminate or at least minimise the effect of weather, particularly when you trade in the Highlands as a construction company.

We haven't seen it yet but with continuing global warming and inclement weather patterns, who knows? Especially in construction projects on the West Coast – this might be an idea that takes off.

Anyway that's the secret here. You need people who are not involved in your industry to try and say from a layman's point of view what they think.

An array of people also joined the Tulloch 'club' in the sense of becoming customers and good people to exchange ideas with, and from the Kevin McCabe camp we spawned a relationship with John Bingham and Peter Dicken of Glass Glover Plc who really had faith in us, in terms of the building and the renovation of their tin shed operations throughout the UK, to facilitate their distribution networks to the large players such as Littlewoods, Safeway, Tesco, etc.

John and Peter took a lot of looking after as they came to Scotland once a week and expected you to be on call to discuss progress on their various projects, but that was to me part of the job.

They were very demanding in terms of their timetabling and blunt. They weren't afraid to reward if a particularly good job was delivered on time as that would benefit their revenue curves.

The headquarters location was in Doncaster where I remember attending frequently, but it was always a hang about exercise until they dealt with the particular fire which was raging within the business at the time and then they came to you, but my view was hey ho they are the customer and I'm a simple servant!

I remember a clear example once when we were bidding for a very large job and they decided not to negotiate with us but to run us against another Scottish contractor.

David Philip and I set off from Scotland very early one morning to travel to Doncaster and 'very early' means 4.30 to 5 o'clock, and we had an interview scheduled for 1 to 2pm.

At the time we had recently become part of Alfred McAlpine Plc and the head of the construction division was one Brian Stanley who, in my recollection, was slightly on the pompous side. As we battled through the A1 and the myriad of motorway connections to get to Doncaster, Mr Stanley had left his Chester office at 12.30, departed McAlpine's airfield at Wrexham and arrived at Doncaster at 1pm just in time for what he thought was an interview with the managing director and operations director of Glass Glover Plc.

If only he had known! John Bingham and Peter Dicken used their usual tactic of having a problem and asking us if we would kindly 'bear with' them. I think bear with them meant 3.30pm!

However Brian Stanley's input was rather tetchy and at the end of the day JB and PD placed the job with us and we beat the mighty Muir Group to this one, which was a good test of our value for money for this burgeoning company called Tulloch as they grew their business throughout the UK.

We became construction problem solvers for Glass Glover, and my favourite subject in those days was the effectiveness of concrete in their yards. The lorries put great pressure on concrete via their axles as they reversed into the dock levellers to facilitate the expeditious loading of the trucks. This caused the concrete to crumble. The solution was to beef up the mix and depth equations of the concrete.

Brian Stanley's report back to head office said that he didn't know why we were working for these guys but our reason was quite simple - we made some money.

On the civils front we enjoyed a series of general managers at the oil fabrication yard at Ardersier which blossomed from relations that started with Donald Tulloch and Bob Matchen and flowed through to Bob Macdonald, Mike Pearson and lastly Don Wright, who was the first Brit to run that yard.

A pivotal figure within the organisation at McDermotts was an individual called TJ Blanchard, a south 'drawl' American who had an armoury of every skill you could think of, but he was really the fixer and we enjoyed a very good relationship with him and, in the close of that process, met Donald Morrison who was head of procurement.

Donald was always interested in your own status within Tulloch, and the first thing he would do after taking his feet off the desk, fag in hand in these days, was to leap up, look out of the window and say 'what are you driving?' I used to have a 5 series BMW which was my pride and joy, but every time I went to see Donald I switched it for a Volvo. I confessed this to him much later when Donald actually joined the Tulloch journey as the sun set on the McDermott era. It was great to be able to tell him he couldn't have a BMW when he joined Tulloch!

111

Cesidio Dicacca was a partner in a firm called Bird Semple in Glasgow and I met him on the other side of a transaction with Kevin McCabe, his client. Cesidio and some others broke away to set up Semple Fraser and out of that Cesidio joined Kevin McCabe's team as their legal counsellor.

I always likened that set up to a New York style business configuration rehearsed in a famous movie, 'The Godfather', and, given that Cesidio had an Italian lineage, he did an excellent job as Kevin's minder from a legal viewpoint only, but whilst he was a legal counsel he also had a good commercial eye for a business and deal and frequently tied up the poor guy on the other side of the deal in knots.

In these days the Scarborough/Teesland Group were growing immensely and the input from people like Cesidio and Steven McBride was highly necessary, but it was also pleasing to see that Kevin's sons, Scott and Simon, began to come through the ranks, and they were really pitched in at the deep end as very young men but fortunately for them we all respected them.

One of their finance people at the time, and the Finance Director prior to Steven McBride was Hillary Cooper.

Picture the scene in a negotiation on a final account when I tried to persuade Hillary over dinner that our financials on this for uplift were well justified and necessary and overdue for payment.

I recall eating at the L'Ariosto restaurant on Michell Street in Glasgow, and as we were in the middle of this negotiation, unknown to me on a Wednesday evening this combo of musicians struck up very good music.

I pitched to Hillary for one last time and said "right the final account is £X, I'm not doing any more work for you unless we agree this."

She did agree and obviously had the necessary empowerment to do so, so I asked her to dance to cement the discussion and agreement!

I think from my point of view that was a first in terms of physically dancing with a client, given that I had danced to clients' tunes on so many occasions, but here was one when we had a very nice waltz in a posh Italian restaurant in the middle of the city of Glasgow – job done. It wasn't always that easy with Hillary so that is probably the only time that I ever won!

Ramsay Johnston was the erudite property director of William Low Plc based in Dundee. We had a standard routine that we visited Ramsay twice a year and never came away without a job to fit our calendar of workload.

We built a great number of Low's supermarkets throughout Scotland and the last one I recall was in the era when Tesco took over Low's and we were awarded a little while before that process a job in Campbelltown to build a William Low, subsequently a Tesco. I still glance at that building every time I pass. Ramsay was kept on with Tesco as a consultant.

At Safeway we had a colleague called Stewart Bates who was the Scottish property director. He gave you the impression that he was an American but he was really British. Stewart's line on every tight Safeway programme in the pre contract meeting was,

'Right let's get our priorities right, when and where is the completion party?'

I remember one completion party for a job in Stornoway being held in Newcastle – yes, Newcastle, and we all had to dress up as vicars to humour Mr Bates, who was of course the cardinal. Anyway, again the old maxim trails out here - the customer is always right.

The relationship with Safeway on the Crossmyloof job mentioned in an earlier chapter was pivotal and I never forget the help given to us by the Safeways property director in London, Gordon Wotherspoon!

Going back to the civil's division we set up a manpower business when manpower started to become tight for North Sea construction operations at Ardersier and out of that we spawned Corrie Industrial Services which supplied welders, pipefitters, engineers etc. throughout the onshore and offshore North Sea business. This business developed to become a worldwide operation long before others. Again it was an example of how you listen to a client's requirements and get on with them.

In the early days of Macgrigor Donald and Tulloch, where you will recall Ian Bankier was a junior partner, we met an individual in the litigation department who was a senior partner called Alasdair Hamilton. Ian Bankier was just out of school and not in the frame on Tulloch as yet.

We had a contractual dispute with Bank of Scotland and needed to sort it.

Alasdair did his usual synopsis of the situation but there was so much money and reputation at stake here I suggested we pay for a QC for a second opinion.

I was politely taken aside by Alasdair Hamilton who explained that he didn't want any QCs on the case and, whilst I was still entitled as client to call for a second opinion, he knew best and better than any QC!

I went along with that and he was proven to be correct in that the deal settled with the Bank of Scotland eventually.

An individual charged with sorting it out, called Herman Mustard, was the general manager at the Bank of Scotland at the time and he was keen to put this behind him, and I recall in a meeting, with Donald Tulloch and me present, an offer was put on the table from the bank for £50K. Neither of us understood whether we had won or lost, were we paying them £50K or were they paying us £50K? We asked for a break, went outside and said 'what the hell do you think? – is it for or against us?' – after all £50K was probably 40% of our profit in these days so a lot was at stake in real terms!

We took the line that we would go back in and look Herman in the eye and say 'Herman, we accept your offer on a no further liability basis' and, from that moment, the relationship with the Bank of Scotland was cemented.

That worked fine for us because we were effectively at fault on that job but the bank clearly wanted to keep us as a client.

Our time at McAlpine's threw up a fascinating range of individual characters in addition to Euan McApline and Tony Scurr who as a leader was a pretty stern individual.

Vic Cooper, a bustling young exec anxious to get to the top was in charge of the energy division which incorporated block manufacture etc., and he certainly had a rocky ride within that division. David Thomson or LDRT to his friends was one of the old professional McAlpine 'man servants' who basically looked after the administration on all their set ups but LDRT was in charge of our minerals division admin and whilst you had to be alert, he was a pussy cat really and most supportive of me as a 'jock' or at least that's what I thought outwardly.

Ivan Abbot was a dinosaur in charge of the black top sections called Alfred McAlpine Asphalt Limited throughout the UK and he had an attitude to business that I didn't like, but there you go, you can't have everybody facing the same way when you are in a company the size of McAlpines.

John Roberts and Owen Rich were the real drivers at the time we joined McAlpine, and these are guys you respected not just from a corporate viewpoint but from an industry viewpoint also.

Smart guys like Philip Davis headed up the housing division but he soon saw the light and bailed out and I came across him in later life when he ran Linden Homes which was subsequently sold to Galliford Try.

Rubbing shoulders with these guys at various conferences in McAlpines was in my book first class, and I thoroughly enjoyed the McAlpine journey and the education.

James McCormack was their legal advisor and I struck up an early good foundation working relationship with James as he was a 'go get and do' man rather than a ditherer. James acted for McAlpine on our management buyout, i.e. the other side, but played it with a square bat which was very helpful.

Indeed later in life James acted for us on one or two situations, until he unfortunately was injured in a serious road accident. He had always liked fast cars and I recall coming up with him to Inverness from Chester to complete the Tulloch deal and thrashing up the road in his RS Cosworth at the time. I remember driving the car through Killiecrankie late one night – wow what an experience.

McAlpine had a finance director called Christopher Edwards. I will never forget that in his room he had the share price monitor. He kept bragging that the ceiling wasn't high enough to accommodate his anticipated share growth!

We used to click in profits at quite a respectable level over the years as their turnover grew and, I bet you when the profit warnings started to happen post 1992, that Christopher's floor wouldn't have had the capacity to cater for the drop in share price – a real case of the share price falling through the floor at Head Office at Hooton on the Wirral – a beautiful location.

However I would say the people in McAlpine were very good to me and I thoroughly enjoyed my stay, and making your stay positive and memorable to me are always the support staff and, whilst I have underpinned the contribution from the various support staff in Inverness, I can't forget Meryl Johns and Janet Wood who gave excellent secretarial support in my stint at Alfred McAlpine Minerals Limited and to young Lisa who used to, on a Sunday, sort out the kitchen so that when I arrived off the overnight sleeper to Crewe at 6 in the morning my breakfast was in the fridge. Thank you Lisa. I will also never forget my going away lunch at the Minerals headquarters in Wrexham when we decided to open Euan McAlpine's wine cellar, and lunch was still going on at 5 o'clock. I really miss these people and included in that is a devoted man called Albert, who, as well as acting as a driver on my many journeys across the English territory, also looked after our interests at our farmhouse in leafy Chester at Tattenhall.

I often wonder where all these characters are in McAlpine and I keep making the effort to contact them, and a year or so ago Anne and I were in South Africa where Tony Scurr now lives but he wasn't in the telephone directory!

It is sad that you lose contact with these people because when you analyze their input it is pretty huge to the Tulloch story.

New arena clients began to emerge over the years and one stands out a mile in the form of Donald MacDonald. We were asked to join with Donald to help to rescue the Aviemore Centre from terminal decline, following a period of ownership with House of Fraser. We had to deal with individuals who simply wanted to rape the facilities for other types of development, other than tourism.

Donald's company at the time was on the main stock market, growing at a fast rate of knots and as part of the process, particularly on the Aviemore deal where it was tortuous, we actually gave up a lot of our client activity that year to be able to deliver this highly demanding programme, to have the whole resort back up and running in a nine month period with support from Bank of Scotland. We even built buildings without planning consent which eventually caught us up but I felt it was very educational for the new National Park as well.

The journey through had its usual challenges but our maxim of always believing the client was right came to the fore again, and we stayed pretty positive with Donald, and did some other work for him after the Aviemore experience all on an amicable, open book basis.

To this day Donald remains a friend and I value his advice in terms of the twists and turns on my corporate journey.

I am pleased to say that Aviemore is back to its former glory (although there is no ice rink there) but it plays such a pivotal part in the Spey Valley tourism curve.

I have rehearsed many banking contacts in the chapters of this tome and I have to say most of my experience was in the BoS era rather than the HBoS era but always having been a Clydesdale or Royal customer I liked the Bank of Scotland ethos when it came to turbulent Corporate conditions.

They, the Bank of Scotland, never failed to step up to the plate and their strapline at the time was 'a friend for life' and that was certainly what was delivered at the coalface when we moved through our various deals with the bank at the core of our funding.

Gavin Masterton I have mentioned and Peter Cummings, Ian Robertson, Ray Robertson, Sandy Cameron, John Barclay, Andy Betchley, Alan Holland - all contributed to the Tulloch journey over the years and Laura Milligan in latter years, God bless her!

Andy Seton was our corporate handler as we moved to the stage of selling our shares to Bank of Scotland for the third time, and I just have to say we in the business arena will probably never see the likes again of the supportive, understanding and commercially proactive staff of the Bank of Scotland who operated in those days.

As we all know the HBoS scenario was borne out of the failed bid to buy Natwest and when you in particular read a book by Ray Perman called Hubris you will understand the real issue which fatally damaged HBoS as the worldwide recession opened up in the Autumn of 2008.

I have had some real challenges with people over the years but I think the most ferocious was with Tony Scurr who had a hot temper and you certainly didn't take him on lightly!

I remember particularly the time when Euan McAlpine was to attend one of his Eton generated stag parties in London but Tony Scurr required a report from him on his desk by 10 o'clock the next morning. Euan asked if I would cover for him, do the report and get it over to Scurr first thing.

I duly did what was requested. Scurr was really angry when he discovered the circumstances, and Ewan and I were both carpeted for this and I thought, unfairly so. Bollocking after bollocking!

Euan was in a different position because he was the Chairman's son but I recall telling Scurr in our offices at Wrexham that I had had enough of this. 'I'm off' I said as I spun on my heels. He told me to stand still so I couldn't resist the retort, 'What do you think this is, the British Army?' I stormed out, into my room, out the escape hatch at the back of the room and meandered home from Wrexham to Inverness.

I caught a flight to Glasgow from Manchester and thereafter a flight to Inverness with every man and his dog chasing me to find out what had happened. I finally got back to Inverness to be met by Anne at the airport saying 'What's wrong?' Euan had phoned the house several times to speak, probably out of guilt.

By Sunday morning it was an 'arm around your shoulder time and meet me on Monday morning' approach by Tony Scurr. He was still volatile and I just wasn't prepared to take it, but a couple of boozy dinners later with Scurr and it was back on track – JB whisky tastes rather nice and Tony Scurr drank a lot of the output of that Scottish bottling plant!

On a personal front many people became good friends such as Andrew Duncan and Jim McBrearty, who started life as a supplier and turned out to be a good golfing partner over the years.

I also met, during my leisure activities, some old school friends and we decided to hold an Inverness Royal Academy year of 1961 forty years on Anniversary Party.

This reunited a lot of people as friends and in particular Ian Lane and Brian Urquhart – it was good to see them all and it is a photograph I look at frequently to see where everybody is – regrettably many people aren't there anymore!

I recently rekindled with social buddies at the doc's club on Ardconnel Terrace and the 'boys' club' and its famous dances (hops) on Planefield Road, Frances Clark, Norma Taylor, Wilma Taylor, Sybil Gerrie, loads more!

Finally my wife and daughters Anne, Caroline and Tina as a family have my fullest admiration and thanks for maintaining a normal family life as I executed my eighty four hour weeks at the helm of Tullochs.

To this day I regularly convene away weekends with my brothers, Anne's family, my children and now grandchildren for get-away sessions so that we maintain the family ethic.

It's great to see the grandchildren at functions like this too, Kirsty, Lewis, Daniel, Finlay and now Jack! Sisters in Law also played a vital role: Helen, Ishbel and Julie. It was gut-wrenching to lose Helen very suddenly in August 2015 – We miss you Helen!

19. HOME SWEET HOME

Building 5,000 houses throughout the UK is no mean feat! from Orkney to Stornoway, Machrahanish, Lanarkshire, Glasgow, Edinburgh, Falkirk, Bute, Dundee, Cumbria, Kent, Surrey, Buckinghamshire, Aberdeen and of course mainland Highland and in particular Inverness, Black Isle, Moray, Nairn, Lochaber, Skye, Golspie, Brora, Dornoch, Dingwall, Forres and Aviemore! Add to that multi million construction and civil projects throughout the UK, contract crushing on a nationwide basis and a vibrant support division of plumbing, electrical and painting and decorating all add to the Tulloch story. Bolt on to that a worldwide manpower agency with offices in Calgary, Belgium, Manchester, Perth WA and a joint venture in Melbourne with Bond Manpower – it all adds up to an exciting mix and clutch of businesses all managed and controlled from Inverness, the capital city of the Highlands of Scotland.

I remember clearly our 'home sweet home' policy propelled Tulloch Homes to become the largest house builder north of Perth, ever!

Superb sales teams, excellent site staff, first class sub contractor base, pro active customer care response units and, most important of all, happy customers. At the peak of economic activity we even sold houses off plan – I need to pinch myself to remember that!

One evening we had a morale boosting sales curry night at the Rajah restaurant in Post Office Lane, Inverness and Lynne Boyd, our Sales Director, mentioned that up to forty cars were queuing for a housing release the next morning at Wester Inshes. We operated a first come first serve policy and the product on offer, two bedroom flats, proved to be very attractive.

In conjunction with the owner of the Rajah we made up forty or fifty carryouts, stunning onion bhajies, pakora, nan bread, rice and curry sauces, improvised with paper plates and plastic cutlery. We made our way up to Wester Inshes where the reception on this very cold winter evening was first class and welcoming.

Ever the pragmatist I thought ahead! I suggested we opened the sales complex for toilet access, so we cleared away Lynne's copious paper trails for privacy purposes, and put a customer designate in charge for the rest of the night until 9am. The customer was Liz Hall from Debenhams who made sure nobody phoned Australia and discreetly didn't abuse our hospitality.

Next morning – bingo – all 50 units sold by 11am and the motto here is 'always think of your customer.'

A house is normally the biggest purchase an individual or family makes and, for Anne and me, it was no different as we recall our own housing journey. The first family house co-incided with our wedding in 1972 and was a one bedroom flat in the vibrant Byres Road area of Glasgow adjacent to the Western Infirmary. We were able to buy this flat off market from one of Anne's nursing colleagues who was moving to Australia so we purchased the property lock stock and barrel, even down to the linen, cutlery and whatever was in the cupboards! It was a barn to heat in winter which was why it wasn't a difficult decision to go to Glendaruel most weekends – meter v bus fare!

We moved back to Inverness in 1974 and purchased a flat at 18 Drynie Terrace. I clearly remember Caroline coming home from Raigmore Hospital as a new born baby to this property. To secure a mortgage in these days you were interviewed by the branch manager of the then locally based and owned building society, and that was daunting.

Drynie Terrace led to 39 Ashie Road, in a leafier suburb of Inverness. This was an end terrace house with a large garden just off Green Drive and our first house as opposed to flat – heaven – your own back door and garden.

From there it was over to the Isle of Skye and a two bedroom bungalow, Ashlee, in the grounds of the Cuillin Hills Hotel adjacent to a magnificent promontory sticking out to sea at Portree Bay called Scorry Breac – great for walking with the pram, at least at lower levels.

From there it was back to the mainland and we purchased a three bedroom MacRae Cedar at 39 Darris Road in Lochardil without seeing it, but the key to me was the schooling at Lochardil Primary School. I remember clearly Caroline's first day at school, departing from this house.

Tina appeared as a baby at this house and I also recall the switch of jobs to Tulloch from this venue. It was then on to Rosebank, 69 Drummond Road at the junction of Stratherrick Road with 4 bedrooms and a patio for the first time! Happy memories at this house including the takeover of Tulloch by McAlpine.

I commuted to Chester from this address leaving Inverness on the Sunday night sleeper at 8pm, being picked up by Albert the driver at 5.30am in Crewe and sitting at my desk by 6.30am – the girls even arranged breakfast for me and a shower was installed in the office to make life easier. On a Friday evening it was the 5pm plane from Manchester to Glasgow and the Loganair boneshaker to Inverness. I wish that service was still on! However after two years of commuting McAlpine's insisted I relocate to the area and we sold Drummond Road and, with assistance from McAplines, bought the magnificent Mill House with its stables, orchard and five bedrooms on the edge of a quaint village called Tattenhall. I also recall we had a conservatory to die for here and good neighbours made our stay very friendly and welcoming.

We were forty minutes to Crewe and thereafter ninety minutes to London, forty minutes from Manchester Airport and the world, and an hour from Alton Towers which pleased the kids.

The MBO appeared and we hot-footed it back to Inverness taking over the Tulloch showhouse at Craig Phadrig whilst Oldtown of Leys Farmhouse was being built, in 12 weeks!

Oldtown of Leys Farmhouse was home for a great number of years and the office within that building witnessed some real change and deal flow on the business journey.

We currently still live on the farm and, as a humble young man from a working class background it is good to be able to enjoy properties in your hometown.

As a family we run a vibrant self-catering business, property based, in stunning locations throughout Scotland with very high standards, and we enjoy the thrill of dealing with the public and receiving repeat business again and again.

20. RELAXATION

How do you relax? You work for Tulloch, you work eighty four hours a week. You're the Chair/MD, you are in charge of strategy, delivery and profits, losses, people, and out of the 84 hours your leisure time is crammed into the weekend.

My farming activities in Argyll and Inverness certainly helped. I was a poor golfer but through Kevin McCabe we were introduced to a golf resort in Spain called La Manga and we owned one house there three times. It was close to Cartagena and I flew in and out of either Alicante or Murcia airports. I perfected a routine. On Thursday late afternoon I left Inverness or Glasgow or London, wherever I happened to be, and I would be in the Piano Bar in La Manga by 9.30 in the evening. Then back to the UK Sunday morning, dinner on Sunday night with the family and back to work Monday, usually 2 or 3 rounds of golf under my belt and a sizzling weekend of good laughs and camaraderie also.

La Manga was buzzing in these days with three golf courses and a range of attractions including world class football facilities which attracted many of the English premiership teams to train there.

I met so many important people there either through golf or through the Piano Bar in the evening and I thought it was time to sell up when I came into the Piano Bar one summer's evening at 9.30ish – the place was mobbed and the guy on the piano – Brian – blasted across the microphone 'Good evening Mr Sutherland' – at that stage I thought it was time I was out of there!

I walked into the same venue another evening on one of my trips and spotted a very tipsy Muir Mackay of Mackay's Garage in Dingwall perched on a bar stool at the very same piano with the same pianist playing away. I passed a note to my friend the piano player saying not to say who it was but playing a request for Mr Muir Mackay from Dingwall – if you can just picture a meerkat in the desert hearing a sound – 'Hello Mr Mackay.' He preened himself and looked round the room with the mannerisms of a meerkat, but what a weekend trip we had. Muir was on a trip with Vauxhall to celebrate good sales figures and we certainly enjoyed ourselves.

It was good craic and I used to meet so many interesting people, even Seve Ballesteros having a coffee in the Lounge. I also met Kenny Dalglish one evening after Inverness Caledonian Thistle had thrashed Celtic 3-1 and basically engineered his and John Barnes sacking 'Hey Marina' called Kenny to his wife 'come and meet the guy who got me the sack.'' We had an excellent chat that evening and Kenny, at least to me, has remained one of the heroes of Scottish football, a nice guy, a nice family and bygones were bygones as was the case largely in football on the subject of Inverness Caledonian Thistle – at least outwardly.

We had two or three Tulloch board meetings in La Manga where we would thank the board for their input in the years we were driving out large profits and I even remember taking the Caley Thistle team in their entirety out there to celebrate a league win in a lower division on a five day break – wow, that took its toll – we stayed in various villas around the resort and trying to marshal all these guys for eating or leisure was a nightmare, particularly as Pele Paterson was our manager, eagerly assisted by Duncan Shearer and excellent at carnage games. Pretty dire events happened that weekend with people being fire hosed out of their beds. We had quite a damage bill at the end of the week.

The golf courses also took a real hammering that week and the top of the piano in the Piano Bar certainly took a tap dancing hammering, as I recall our respected manager dancing on top of it singing his heart out.

Sadly, as I indicated, we sold up La Manga in the early part of the new century and all I have now are the memories of Victors which was a really up market restaurant which always flew the Inverness Caledonian Thistle pennant, alongside the pennants of many of the premiership clubs in England. One of the bars in the square, would you believe, had a Clachnacuddin shirt framed as well as a Caley Thistle one. I never found out who the Clachnacuddin visitor was.

Anyway, not a good golfer is how I would describe my golfing even though I had plenty of practice in Spain, and this persists to this day, but I do enjoy it. If I was however a golf course designer, mine would be designed on 10 holes as 18 took up so much time.

Watching the kids grow up, following on to tertiary education, has been excellent relaxation with a tinge of worry! Five grandchildren now at a fast rate of noughts is the order of the day for relaxation and it really is most pleasurable to see Kirsty, Lewis, Daniel, Finlay and Jack begin their journeys in life with Kirsty and Lewis now very communicative in their speech patterns which I thoroughly enjoy – I have to say with them whilst it's hard work it's very relaxing.

The farm activity in Inverness, where we have one hundred or so cattle and sheep, is my idea of stress-busting, but not for much longer

Anne and I built the farming business up. Our farming activities were borne out of buying Anne's home in Glendaruel which was called Home Farm, and was the local dairy farm, from her brother Alasdair, who inherited the farm before the death of Anne's mother.

Alasdair however saw his life in Australia more than in Scotland and moved out there, but needed the farm to pay his dowry to marry an Australian girl, and a much bigger dairy operation than the one in Scotland was on offer. Who could stand in this young man's way?

To finance the farm we bought cattle in Dalmally in March, took them back to Glendaruel, grazed them and sold them in September/October and sold them at a profit sufficient to pay the interest. So that's how we got our interest in farming. A big thank you to John Ligerwood at Clydesdale Bank for his faith in this project!

However working in the early days on the farm feeding, and buying silage and straw was very heartening and, every time I go to visit Alasdair in Australia, the first thing I do is head for the byre to see what's happening with the cows – four hundred being milked now for market products exclusively.

We currently own Culduthel and Oldtown Farms in Inverness and have started a plan to develop some of the land but we have built up the farming operations to a level where we have become recognised breeders of Highland cattle, indeed winning the last Royal Smithfield. Our expert neighbours in breeding Highland cattle, at Leys Castle, the Walker family, via their nephew Michael Williamson, never forgave us. We had managed to achieve in five years what their ancestors had tried to achieve in fifty years.

However getting older and pulling yourself up into a tractor every day gets harder and harder but I suppose that's life.

An aside here is that when Anne and Rhona were young in Glendaruel, you had to work hard on the farm. you weren't allowed to sit back and do nothing, and given it was a seven day operation, and given how intense a milking operation was, Anne and Rhona vowed that they would never marry a farmer!

Rhona married a geologist, Ian Goodenough. Anne now says that she has married a farmer by default.

When you look back at the hard work their parents put in at Home Farm and Glendaruel they nevertheless were never short of anything and they had a lifestyle which they obviously enjoyed very much.

There were some pretty hairy moments in farming at Oldtown. I recall one evening, when Bob Tulloch had a night off, I phoned Bob to say that one of the maiden Highlanders was calving. Bob came across and we immediately got some help from Hughie Munro at Leys Castle. I've never seen this before but the Highlander was actually on its hind quarters trying to pin these guys to the shed wall, it was so ferocious.

In came the cavalry in the form of John Crilley, the cattleman at Leys, who had a reputation for being a beast whisperer or so he thought! John, Whisper!

The cow was still on its hind quarters when John arrived and I remember sending Anne into the house because I thought if the cow broke out we would have a real problem.

However John persevered and lassoed it, but in the meantime I had phoned the vet to ask if a mad cow could be shot even though the beast was deep in calf, but fortunately JC brought it under control and the beast calved. We immediately sold it, cow and calf, disclosing to the purchaser the degree of difficulty we had had. John Wayne would have been very proud of John Crilley! The purchaser didn't keep the beast long either, wise man.

Skiing was another relaxation because it was something we could do together as a family and we have had many trips to Europe, America and Switzerland in particular and to me it was much more attractive than lying on a beach.

Anne and I still go to Switzerland as a friendship developed with one of our joint venture partners. Ferdinand and Dorly Hinterreger were partners in the Royal Marine in Brora and knew all the good resorts in Switzerland, so we have been using their expertise to enjoy ourselves over the last few years.

However in life I have met so many people who have been most helpful and, whilst everybody is out to make a buck for themselves, there was a camaraderie in business which I think was positive and necessary.

To return to charity work. This also was stress busting activity for me, and we had some spectacular fundraisers in the early days even auctioning houses to try and pay for a British Heart Foundation rehabilitation centre at Raigmore hospital for Dr Finlay Kerr's department and many other fundraising events too numerous to mention.

I always took the view that people were less fortunate than us and whilst the National Health Service does a sterling job they also needed support and help.

Everybody will be aware of the usual format at these dinners where you had an auction and when Douggie McGillivray and I were at the dinner the organisers always rubbed their hands because we had this 'game' of trying to bid things up.

Our technique was never to try and buy them ourselves but to see somebody else come through the middle of the defence. On many many occasions that didn't work and one of us would pick up something vastly over priced but for a good cause!

The Homeless Trust started life as the Highland Homeless at Christmas Trust and along with Alan Sellar and David Stewart, our MSP, I helped set it up. When we first set sail in a portacabin within a building in King Street we were told by all the authorities that there wasn't a homeless problem in Inverness – wow.

Thereafter we borrowed premises and used portacabins internally to house our guests from cold winter nights and we had the support of Inverness churches, Salvation Army, Raigmore Hospital, Porterfield Prison, Northern Constabulary, Marks and Spencer and a myriad of other supporters. We eventually set up a homeless centre at Waterloo Place in Inverness with my previous employer, Tulloch, donating that to the Homeless Trust and it was humbling when we were really housing people on cold winter nights on camp beds with sleeping bags when somebody would turn to you and say 'Hello David' – a school friend who had hit hard times but that happened frequently.

Relaxing sometimes work, and thinking that my malignant melanoma was my wake up call to slow down in more recent times, in 2012 I suffered a condition called a left 'non arteritic anterior ischemic optic neuropathy.' This was simply a stroke which hit the back of my left eye and caused me to lose three quarters of my eye sight with no rectification possible and a real lifestyle warning from the doctors.

My message to people in a similar situation is: you need to smell the roses, look after yourself and exercise. I should really have heeded these words when I was running at 100 miles an hour in business!

21. NEW YORK NEW YORK

Extract from the Inverness Courier:

I love the song 'Empire State of Mind' by Alcia Keys and Jay Z of rapper fame, and given that we literally risked life and limb to walk the 26+ miles of the New York marathon, I thought it was important to reproduce part of the blog I wrote and published in the Inverness Courier recounting the process. Catriona Cameron and I are eternally grateful to Dunkin Doughnut because the sugar rush we received from partaking of their product range with a steamy cup of coffee at the half way mark on the New York marathon inspired us to move on and complete the process though cold, irritable, hypothermic and shattered.

Read the blog as this tells the true story of the build-up, the angst, the elation and the realisation that we raised a lot of money to help improve the facilities for sick children at Raigmore Hospital in Inverness through the Archie Foundation.

'1. That's the way to do it

Not long now before the big day on 6th November and I've been getting more miles in. But the closer it comes, the more daunting it seems to me.

'Last week, I did the West Island Way, seven and a half miles across Bute in the teeth of a howling gale, seeing the submarines and warships make their way along the Firth of Clyde and finishing down in the valley past the ruined sixth century Celtic chapel of St Blanes on which a 12th Century Norman church, also ruined, was built.

'That means I've completed a hat-trick of Great Glen Way, West Island Way and Cowal Way and such walking routes are a great asset to their communities. My walk from Muirtown Bridge to Dochgarroch and back on the other side of the canal was a great reminder of the scenic value of this underused route and British Waterways deserve credit for looking at further popularising the canal.

'This weekend coming, I plan to do a circular walk of Glen Affric, some 13 miles along with my 'coach' Andrew Duncan, the accountant. I've been grateful for his company on my walking expeditions despite the fact that he's a Ross County fan who kept telling me how well they are playing and how they'll be in the SPL next season and stay there!

'As well as pounding the Affric trails by the ancient Caledonian Forest, I'll be walking later in the week at Tomfat Woods and Inverarnie. Both picturesque walks just outside the city.

'I read about the 100 year old Sikh man from London who completed a marathon in Toronto. How's that for putting the pressure on me? But he's a good few stones slimmer than me and my target is to get to at least 13 miles in New

York which is the trigger for all my sponsors having to stump up for the ARCHIE Appeal.

'I had a health check last week and they say I'm not fit but I'm not un-fit enough not to be allowed to make the effort. I also had a second visit to Caley Thistle's excellent physio John McCreadie who's supplied me with all the necessary ointments.

'But after such an early report to the Park, I'm told that those of us who are walking have a start time of 10.30am, which is 1am in Inverness time. After the elite athletes begin racing, there is a two hour trudge forward for those of us in the rear-guard just to get to the start line. That'll be an endurance test in itself. I think I'll go down the night before and put my towel on the start line!

'Catriona Cameron, owner of the Mustard Seed and the Kitchen restaurants in Inverness, will be walking with me through those vast canyons of Manhattan and beyond. But there are five hardier, fitter Inverness folk who will be running the marathon for ARCHIE.

'Valerie Matheson is a nurse at the Breast Care Centre while Lorna Mackenzie is a nurse in Ward 11 in Raigmore. Laura Mackintosh, my astonishingly fit personal assistant and mother of two, ran the recent Monster Challenge and did the Great Glen Way last weekend.

'Neil Cameron, Catriona's husband, is also running, as is Northern Constabulary officer Tony Anderson who I suppose has experience of pounding a beat!

'These brave and determined runners have my great admiration as they set off for such a good cause.

'Four of the Appeal management team in Aberdeen are also running, making a total of 11 of us setting forth to raise funds towards the £1 million appeal to give Raigmore Hospital a state-of-the-art childrens ward.

'We've all been tracking the weather in the Big Apple and right now it's looking good with 55 degrees forecast for the marathon. That's a bit warmer than we've been having it in Inverness!

'So at least we shouldn't freeze. But the clock is running down and the nerves are beginning to kick in. The city that never sleeps is beckoning.....

'2. It's the Final Countdown

'I fly across the Atlantic this Friday and 'New York, New York' awaits as the Archie team gets ready to line up for the 41st New York Marathon.

'There were only 120 runners for the first one and less than half of them finished. It did not become a huge event until the sixth year when the route was altered to go through all five boroughs – Manhattan, Brooklyn, Queens, the Bronx and Staten Island. By 1978 there were 9000 competitors and it has kept growing from then to the point where last year 45,350 took part and two million spectators lined the route, at least we won't be lonely.....

'After some hard walking in recent weeks, this last week is all about easy walking, not overdoing it and ensuring I don't pick up an injury which prevents me from getting to that start line at the Verrazano Narrows Bridge in Staten Island.

'My personal goal, as I've emphasised from day one, is to walk at least 13 miles and cross the Pulaski Bridge, leaving Brooklyn and entering Queens, which is the halfway mark, and this trigger £10,000 of personal sponsorship for the Archie Appeal, towards giving Raigmore Hospital, and the Highlands, a state-of-the-art childrens ward and treatment facility. I'm very pleased to have received personal donations from as far apart as London and Caithness.

'I certainly hope to get further than 13 miles, but that's when the cash is guaranteed. Mind you, in last year's event the Olympic gold medallist Hailie Gebresillassie only managed halfway before a knee problem ended his challenge.

'The rest of the Archie Highland team will raise £3000 each so if we all meet our race targets then we'll rake in £25,000, which would be a marvellous boost to the Appeal coffers.

'Lifescan have given me a huge pack of Johnston and Johnston athlete aids for our team including blister plasters, foot gel and the like and that's a nice gesture.

'Saturday is all about a quiet reconnoitre of the route, do a bit of easy walking to relieve any muscle knots caused by the transatlantic trip, get over any jet lag and just relax and gather ourselves for the big day. Fluid intake and energy storage is so vital for such a challenge as is carbohydrate intake.

'During my training regime I've learned more about things like tendons, Achilles and muscles I didn't know I had. As I drag my portly frame along the route, I hope they all hold up. I'd hate to blow a gasket!

'I'd love to get to the finish line at Central Park but I know that's six miles further than I've ever walked before so I'm not counting my chickens. I'll settle for reaching halfway, ensuring my sponsorship kicks in, and then see how many muscles are screaming as I try to move on from there.

'The myriad of letters and emails I've received wishing me well has been quite humbling. I'll do my best and we'll see how far that takes me in the city that never sleeps. I reckon I'll have no bother sleeping on Sunday night!

'3. A lot of air miles on a direct Continental Airways flight to New York to run or walk 13 or 26 miles puts it in perspective. Edinburgh and Scotland are lucky to have this flight and global connectivity. Why don't we in Inverness have a connector to our capital?

'Half way the pilot called our attention to a spectacular sight to the right. A completely ice free Greenland. What a sight and underpinning global warming statistics. Our arrival in New York was spectacular circling the city and marvelling at the skyscrapers protruding into the sky and between the city and hinterland housing a population of 8.5 million people, 25% watching us on Sunday. Our downtown hotel near Time Square housed the entire team, Lorna, Lorraine, Laura, Tony, Neil and Catriona and from this base we met the American Scottish Foundation who have taken Archie under their wing this weekend endorsing and hopefully contributing to our mission of raising money to improve the facilities at Raigmore's children's ward to match the excellent medical, nursing and support care for our younger citizens.

'In the late afternoon we prepared for the Parade of Nations in Central Park, a very cold Central Park, but warmed by the reception we received from all nations photographing relentlessly our kilts. Venezuela, Japan, South Africa, Oz were all in good spirits. A final barter with a steward persuaded him that whilst we marched in solidarity with the

United Kingdom we were a nation within the union and we marched 10 feet behind with our own flags and all the Scottish recruits we enrolled from the crowd helped us. Alex Salmond and David Cameron would have been proud of us!

'Our American Scottish Foundation colleagues were excellent assists during the day and the Chairman, Alan Bain, who operates a Harris Tweed mill even came to help us. He told us he was on his way to Scotland to visit his business but made sure he stayed to help us as he understood the Archie Foundation aims in terms of the Raigmore hospital appeal. The foundation has had a long week of activities with it's Lord Smith of Kelvin picking up another prestigious award for his business acumen in the form of the association's Wallace prize. Also a new Scottish tartan shop opened in the shopping drag which went down a bomb with locals and tourists alike.

'On Saturday night we visited the St Andrews restaurant, a Scottish restaurant, just off Times Square and 53 people from the American Scottish Foundation and the Archie Foundation both Inverness and Aberdeen were in attendance, with the Archie marathon team being the guests of honour. The event was kindly sponsored by BP and it's North American director, Trevor Garlick, who attended in person which was a real boost.

'However, following good practice the evening was curtailed to enable everyone to get a night's sleep prior to the Sunday morning challenge.

'Mornings in New York are crisp and cold at present and it was no different at 6am aiming for a 10ish start from Staten Island. However express porridge and space food kept us quiet when queuing but on this occasion; the queue was forty thousand people.

'All our team achieved their objectives and between the silent auction and sponsorship we raised £40K plus the whole weekend for Archie including all 47 runners made a total £180K between Grampian and Highland. This was an excellent result for both Grampian and the Highland appeal.

'Perhaps next year we will encourage more highland runners and up the odds slightly.

'It's over, there has been good banter and camaraderie among runners from all nations and New York produced a real community effort to stage this event.

'It truly is the city that never sleeps but I'd sum it up more succinctly as the city that never stands still.

'Well done to all our Highland runners and everyone is looking forward to competing again next year in one of the world's greatest marathons in one of the world's greatest cities.

'As for a self-confessed portly gentleman from Inverness I think I'll stick to the spectacular scenery of Glen Affric and the likes as, at 62, I felt a little over awed by the spectacle of supremely fit people running this marathon either to prove it to themselves or more importantly to raise money for important charities.

'Well done to all 43,000 participants.

'I've vowed to keep up my training over the winter so that I might be able to drop the word portly if I'm mad enough to take up some other challenge in the future.

'However the experience has been fantastic for all of us, everyone calling themselves New Yorkers were first class in supporting our endeavours and many of us will return to fight the fight in years ahead.

'However, from the Archie foundation's Highland appeal we have augmented our coffers assisting us towards our goal of raising £1M to make the difference at the children's ward housed in Raigmore hospital.

'4. Big Man in the Big Apple

'My blistered feet, with the help of the casualty department at Raigmore hospital, are on the mend after pounding the streets of New York for the eight hours 20 minutes it took Inverness restaurant owner Catriona Cameron and myself to walk the 26 mile route.

'It was gruelling but an unforgettable experience, well worth flying the 6500 mile round trip from Edinburgh to the Big Apple to be among the 48,000 participants who raised a collective 34 million dollars for charitable causes.

'When we arrived home my feet were in pretty poor shape and I've had to walk gingerly for a few days – each ache and pain a reminder of tramping through the five boroughs of the city that never sleeps.

'All the Archie Inverness team did magnificently – the first home, running the route in a splendid three hours 56 minutes apiece were Valerie Matheson of the Breast Care Clinic and Northern Constabulary officer Tony Anderson.

'Neil Cameron, husband of Catriona, hit the finish line in 4 hours 28 minutes, just ahead of Laura Mackintosh, who did superbly in her first marathon with a finish in 4 hours 30 minutes. Only two minutes behind her was Lorna Mackenzie, the nurse from Raigmore hospital Ward 11.

'Our Inverness septet raised a total of £40,000 towards Archie's goal of a £1 million new state-of-the-art childrens facility for Raigmore. Added to that is £28,000 we raised at a Silent Auction at Drumossie Hotel a couple of nights before our departure. Next year, we hope to do a bit of recruiting and build on this year's marathon success by fielding a larger Archie team. Anyone interested? Let us know.

'On our flight over, the pilot called our attention to a spectacular sight – a completely ice free Greenland. What a sight, underpinning global warming statistics. And flying in to New York, with its 8.5 million people and spectacular skyline, gave our team a real lift and a reminder of our task.

'There was a pre-race parade of nations in Central Park on the Friday night and while we were proud to be within the UK contingent, we did manage to create a 10ft gap and march behind the saltire and the flag of the American Scottish Foundation who we had dinner with that evening. Its Chairman, Alan Bain, has a Harris Tweed mill in Carloway, Lewis, and we remain hopeful that they can assist the Archie Appeal. At the parade we met Ron Hill, the well-known former British long distance runner who won the gold medal in the Commonwealth Games marathon in Edinburgh in 1970.

'Getting up so early on Sunday morning to be at the race start by 6.30am New York time was vastly different from my normal Sunday wake-up time. The best way to get to the start was to take the Staten Island ferry which passes very close to the Statue of Liberty, so that was a splendid way to set us on our way.

'We walkers were allocated to our corral and the wait to get started enabled Catriona and I to grab sustenance in the form of a coffee and bagel. At 10.45am sharp, a canon boomed, and that was us off, walking across the Verazano

Narrows Bridge which took us from Staten Island into the mainland of the city. We became friendly with a lady from Germany who was tackling the marathon as a gift to herself on her 60th birthday and she stayed with us most of the way and we were pleased that she also made it to the finish.

'Two million spectators lined the route and gave terrific encouragement. We had our names, the charity and the Scottish flag on our T-shirts and quite a few shouted specific backing. That helped put a spring in our steps, particularly walking through Brooklyn where there was massive cheering from huge crowds.

'Competitors took advantage of the refreshment stations where you could take on board water and energy gel. These were tubes of liquid food you squeezed down as you walked. I have to say that liquidised apple strudel doesn't taste the same on the hoof!

'Because we walkers were so far behind the runners, by the time we hit the Williamsburg Bridge, 10 miles out, the refreshment stations had stopped and the stations were being dismantled, which was a bit of a disappointment. But when we reached the halfway mark that cheered us up again as it meant our sponsorship would be paid. Catriona and I celebrated with a quick pit stop to a Dunkin Doughnuts for a jam doughnut and a coffee, consumed as we walked, and it was this wee caffeine lift which led to us discussing how we felt and deciding we would go for it and try for the finish.

'When we crossed the Queensboro Bridge, the whole horror of what lay ahead met our eyes as we could see how far we had to go. That took us into the Bronx, a notoriously rough, tough borough – and here, things changed drastically, with few spectators but a policeman every 30 yards. They were quite obviously there to prevent competitors from coming to harm or wandering down a dangerous street.

'From the Bronx, we walked through Harlem and the support and encouragement from the side lines returned. A musical group on the pavement played 'Imagine' and we sang the John Lennon anthem as we walked along. Yet another band played 'These Boots Were Made for Walking' and again we joined in lustily. Through Manhattan we trooped and a sign told us we'd covered 20 miles.

'It was here, however, that the gathering chill took its effect on us. Coldness clicked in through our bodies and as we reached Fifth Avenue, I asked a policeman what the temperature was and he said four degrees. That was a difficult time for us as we shivered and wondered if we had pushed ourselves too far. But we plugged on and when the welcome sight of Central Park met our eyes we again chatted and decided to up the anti and go faster, on the basis that would give us more heat. So we mustered a small jog as we completed the lap of the famous park and kept that up all the way to the finish line.

'I felt slightly delirious with the cold and when someone from the marathon support team handed me a blanket it was hugely welcome. Collecting my medal at the time took second priority to wrapping myself in that blanket.

'Once I warmed up, my own feeling was one of double relief – that I'd managed to go all the way and that it was all over. My feet were so sore that a kind helper took me on a golf buggy the quarter mile to the taxi rank and he even refused a tip I'd been very willing to pay.

'Team Archie Inverness may have triumphed but we certainly didn't celebrate. There was no hitting the bright lights for us. In fact, we didn't even eat dinner, I couldn't face food. All I wanted – after my blisters were treated – was my bed which I exhaustedly struggled into at 9.30pm. I didn't need rocking.

'Next morning though, we were hale and hearty and starving and consumed a full breakfast with lashings of toast, coffee and orange juice. And no walking – bliss. Then, it was off for Team Archie's courtesy call on the UK Consul General to New, York, Danny Lopez, who had also run the marathon the day before. I passed on greetings from Jimmy Gray, Provost of Inverness.

'My wife Anne didn't know that I'd gone the distance until I phoned her. But technology is wonderful these days and there is an iPhone app which enabled some supporters back in Inverness to track the Team Archie members in the marathon on a mile by mile basis. Amazing!

'If it were not for Catriona's companionship and constant cajoling, I don't think I'd have gone the full 26 miles. Because I'd left it so late before deciding I'd complete, I simply hadn't done sufficient preparation. At the age of 62 and carrying rather too much weight, that risked making it 'Mission Impossible' but I got there. If I do another marathon in 2012 then I realise I'll have to have much more preparation than this time.

'New York gained a huge economic boost from the race, with every hotel full, and the city did a magnificent job while the cheers from New Yorkers, and the changes of my name, are something that will stay with me.

'I'm pleased my body stood up to the test, but the greatest pleasure is that our Magnificent Seven rode in to town and rode out with £40,000 in sponsorship strapped to our saddlebags. Superbly done to Catriona, Valerie, Tony, Laura, Neil and Lorna – I'm enormously proud of you all. My aim as Chairman of the Archie Appeal Highland is to reach our £1 million target by the end of 2012. We can then look back on our New York achievement and adventure and think: "We did our bit in the Big Apple". '

Clifton
Passaic
Fort Lee
Caldwell
Verona
Wallington
Glen Co
Manorhaven
Port Washington
West Orange
Nutley
Cliffside Park
Livingston
Bloomfield
Belleville
North Bergen
Great Neck
East Hill
Union City
Great Neck Plaza
Roslyn Heigh
East Orange
Kearny
Mineola
South Orange
Hoboken
North New Hyde Park
Garden Ci
Irvington
Newark
New York
Franklin Square
Hempst
Union
Hillside
South Richmond Hill
Kenilworth
Elizabeth
Bayonne
Upper New York Bay
Valley Stream
Clark
Linden
Woodmere
Oceansid
Rahway
Jamaica Bay
Inwood
Staten Island
Coney Island
Long Beach
Iselin
Carteret
Rockaway Park
Woodbridge
5 miles
10 km
Fords
© 2011 Microsoft Corporation © 2010 NAVTEQ

22   POLITICAL LANDSCAPE

To us Scots, particularly Scots in the Highlands, it has been an interesting period of landscape issues on the political front, basically leading up to the Referendum in 2014, nearly two years of relative stagnation for Scotland as all attention was diverted to this aspect of our day-to-day lives.

I knew the personalities on both sides of the equation and whether it was the status quo or Independence, I made my view clear about having differing rates of taxation for example and the impact that would have on Scottish businesses, and I didn't hesitate to say so a number of years ago.

However, there are some unsung heroes in this debate for our collective future and I think one of these heroes is Sir Ian Wood, who had the guts to stand up and say that in his opinion, and having worked in the oil industry for over 40 years, he saw danger ahead in terms of the oil price and to build a sustainable exchequer function on the back of that would be dangerous. He was attacked, ridiculed and cast aside by certain politicians, but hey presto, not that long after the Referendum, the price crashed and we are now being told by the oil experts that we have to get used to $60 or less a barrel for oil and the impact that will have on all the job creating activities spinning out from the North Sea.

I'd like to say thank you to Sir Ian for pointing all this out to us and for having the guts to stand up and do so in the public domain.

Tales of intimidation and threats abound and the Press have not been backward in coming forward with these, but you've got to respect the views on both sides of the spectrum and there is no doubt that on the 'YES' side there was passion and on the 'NO' side a drive to maintain the status-quo.

However, what we've all got to bear in mind is that we need a stable Scotland, with proper economic policies, and the idea of devolution being delivered via the Smith Commission report is appealing to a lot of people here and, I have to say, listening to the debates around the Westminster and Scottish Parliaments currently, particularly on the subject of full fiscal autonomy, it is clear that our Nationalist colleagues do not wish to have this status to manage at present, but who knows down the line?

Land reform also began to appear on the agenda, and I think what's being produced doesn't recognise the contribution estates, farms, etc make to the local rural communities and we do risk depopulation particularly I think in areas of the Western Isles, North West Scotland and parts of Argyll.

However, to round off the political issues, I though the day following the Referendum Alex Salmond was acting in a statesman-like way by tendering his resignation, particularly as he'd said prior to the Referendum, that one vote would do it either way and that was it for a lifetime. Shortlived!

We don't want to get embroiled in endless fights and battles about our status – we are part of the United Kingdom, we need the United Kingdom particularly in trying times but it is also good that the political establishment in the UK recognises that the countries of Scotland, Wales and Northern Ireland are capable of managing more devolved powers.

One of my very avid SNP friends, following the Referendum, said to me 'I voted for change and one way or the other I got it.'

'Good response' I replied and we shook hands, and I said 'Let's get on with it.'

That's the attitude to have and let's hope the people of Scotland feel the same way!

22. CONCLUSION

I've spent more than 31 years in one job which sounds impressive until you realise that it's overshadowed by Tulloch's corporate journey of almost 90 years! Born as a humble company and riding numerous crises to maintain success, the Tulloch journey has been positive, memorable, and exceptionally worthwhile.

The company has come such an incredibly long way. For me, the journey is now complete. I hope that the business that has been created will continue to flourish, or morph into some other workable, profitable, format.

I stepped down in November 2011 basically at the request of Lloyds Banking Group in Spring 2011 who wished to signal change and I agreed to the request given that to reject would have been catastrophic for Tulloch and the good people who work within the business.

I really enjoyed the years of mutual trust between HBoS, BoS and myself. But, in turn, I also recognise that Lloyds Banking Group had to look after their own financial health within the banking sector. They certainly had their challenges to deal with.

Attacking the banks in political terms to me is not good as we need all the banks in the UK to contribute and be the engines of the economy, particularly supporting SMEs and business units such as ours. However, when asked I still assist Tulloch and no doubt there is a final chapter around the corner, but all credit to LBG for staying the course with Tulloch.

I have made a very comfortable living from Tulloch, but in many ways I paid a high price by sacrificing aspects of my personal life. I think I found a good balance in my family life over the years. If my daughters, Caroline and Tina, were ever denied my full attention it was more than made up for by Anne who is an amazing mother, wife and friend, who has a fantastic ability to keep your feet on the ground and bring you back to earth when necessary.

Thank you Highlands of Scotland (and the rest of the UK!) for the opportunity to be of service. Thank you to all the teams, bankers, customers, friends, local government colleagues, politicians, and everyone else who has ever contributed to our corporate success. I see all business as an opportunity to create profit or tangible benefits. Tulloch has created thousands of jobs and delivered training to thousands of young apprentices. The company has created buoyancy and vibrancy in the community here and throughout Scotland.

I counted it up. We employed over 1,500 people at peak and 2,000 direct sub contractor employees. We generated significant profits with a solid charitable giving ethic. We built in excess of 5,000 houses throughout the UK and built landmark buildings of all sorts, again across the UK. We regularly received criticism of our house designs from architectural sources, but these critics failed to recognise that house building had to be linked to price envelopes so that people could afford to buy them and live within them - nothing wrong with that and anyway in my mind critics who dip in and out of markets they don't understand should keep quiet.

I now welcome the opportunity to spend more time with my extended private corporate family companies, and to enjoy the stunning self-catering business that we created from the very basics in Glendaruel. It now also trades at a high level in Brora, Isle of Skye and Inverness.

I love the family farming activities that we operate in Inverness, thanks to the hard graft of those around me. My family is a wonderful source of strength and I already have five very active grand-children. I have no idea what line of business they will choose to enter. My only hope is that they follow their hearts and their dreams so that they make a truly authentic living in the world.

I'm inspired by the enthusiasm and business acumen that I can see around me in the Highlands. There are some amazingly gifted people here who just need a little confidence and conviction to help them on their way. I've already had a few unofficial approaches from individuals seeking business advice. Whilst I don't envisage a position akin to the *Dragon's Den* anytime soon I am happy to share my knowledge. As much as I love walking the dogs and devouring the newspapers I can't see myself living out that role on a full time basis. I'm much happier scrutinising ideas and how to take them forward.

People in the Highlands have helped to make my business journey exciting so it is with heartfelt gratitude that I am willing to support the next generation in the boardroom take that first step.

Errors of judgement or unexpected results are part of the package in business and I think to some extent the current economic climate has made people terrified to stand too close to the precipice. You can learn from any failure. It is only if you keep repeating the process without learning that it becomes a mistake.

Thomas Edison invented the light bulb after thousands of attempts. He maintained that: 'I haven't failed. I've found 10,000 ways not to make a light bulb.' Many of life's failures are people who did not realise how close they were to success when they gave up. Our greatest weakness lies in giving up. The most certain way to succeed is always to try just one more time. I think that's true, and my advice in business would always be to put all your energy behind your idea and drive it forward with passion and conviction. A successful business life is available to everyone if that is their focus. And, remember what I said about your bankers; stay close because without their support you do not have a business. I am very grateful for the support throughout the years from HBoS, LBG, Royal Bank of Scotland, and Clydesdale Bank who have all provided excellent support throughout my career.

Finally let's forget about banks and think positively by concentrating on people and ideas, and I would have to say that the Highlands, Scotland and the UK are still abuzz with ideas and looking forward to the much heralded corporate recovery which will occur particularly if we help the smaller business units to survive. Big business does okay so come on UK Government, help the entrepreneurial spirit come alive at a faster rate. I have really enjoyed the modest contribution I think I've made to the Highlands of Scotland which is a beautiful place to live, an excellent place to visit or do business, and is an exceptional platform to trade from within the UK and worldwide.

I am proud to be a Highlander with Wick roots, an Inverness pedigree and a deep love for Argyll, and I hope my telling of the Tulloch story helps to inspire others to undertake similar challenges. Whilst always being understanding of the challenges and difficulties of others, remember that, in all you do, doing one's best is all that can be expected.